PR-10042

hw.design gmbh
Türkenstraße 55 – 57
80799 München

Ranking:Design 2002/2003 – Die 100 Besten / *The Top 100*

Ranking:Design 2002/2003 – Die 100 Besten / *The Top 100*

Ranking : Design

2002/2003

Industrie-Design

Hersteller

Industrial Design

Manufacturers

Die 100 Besten *The Top 100*

Impressum/*Imprint*

Herausgeber/*Editor*
Dr.-Ing. Alex Buck
R:D Publishing Concepts AG
Ludwigstraße 12
D-63067 Offenbach am Main
Telefon/*Phone*
+49 (0)69/800 57 57
Telefax/*Fax*
+49 (0)069/800 57 59
E-mail/*E-mail*
hk@rdpc.de
Internet/*Website*
www.ranking-design.de
Konzeption/*Conception*
R:D Publishing Concepts AG
Projektleitung/*Project Management*
Heike Kleffmann

Verlag/*Publisher*
Schäffer-Poeschel Verlag
für Wirtschaft · Steuern · Recht GmbH & Co. KG
Werastraße 21-23
D-70182 Stuttgart
Telefon/*Phone*
+49 (0)711/21 94-0
Telefax/*Fax*
+49 (0)711/21 94-119
E-mail/*E-mail*
info@schaeffer-poeschel.de
Internet/*Website*
www.schaeffer-poeschel.de

Druck/*Printing*
Wilhelm Bing Druckerei und Verlag GmbH
Briloner Landstraße 60
D-34497 Korbach
Telefon/*Phone*
+49 (0)5631/97 17-0
Telefax/*Fax*
+49 (0)5631/97 17-80
E-mail/*E-mail*
info@druckerei-bing.de
Internet/*Website*
www.druckerei-bing.de

Die Deutsche Bibliothek – CIP-Einheitsaufnahme
Ein Titeldatensatz für diese Publikation ist bei der
Deutschen Bibliothek erhältlich
ISBN 3-7910-2216-4

© R:D Publishing Concepts AG
Printed in Germany
April/2003

Alle Rechte vorbehalten, besonders die der
Übersetzung in fremde Sprachen.
All rights reserve, especially the rights to
translation into other languages.

Inhalt/
Content

- 7 — Über das Ranking:Design/
  About Ranking:Design

- 9 — Die Methode/
  The Method

- 11 — Vorwort/
  Preface

**Ranking:Design
Die 100 Besten/Industrie-Design**
The Top 100/Industrial Design

- 19 — Handwerk und Industrie/
  Trade and Industry

- 25 — Medizin und Rehabilitation/
  Medicine and Rehabilitation

- 31 — Medien, Kommunikation und Unterhaltungselektronik/
  Media, Communication and Entertainment Electronics

- 33 — Verkehrsmittel und Sonderfahrzeuge/
  Transportation and Special Use Vehicles

- 39 — Büro und Objekt/
  Office and Public Space

- 41 — Wohnung/
  Living

- 47 — Haushalt, Küche und Bad/
  Household, Kitchen and Bathroom

- 59 — Public Design/
  Public Design

- 61 — Freizeit, Sport und Spiel/
  Leisure, Sport and Play

- 67 — Accessoires/
  Accessories

- 69 — Gesamt-Ranking: Top 20/
  Overall Ranking: Top 20

- 77 — Hall of Fame Industrie-Design/
  Hall of Fame Industrial Design

- 81 — Adressen Industrie-Design/
  Addresses Industrial Design

**Ranking:Design
Die 100 Besten/Hersteller**
The Top 100/Manufacturers

- 89 — Handwerk und Industrie/
  Trade and Industry

- 95 — Medizin und Rehabilitation/
  Medicine and Rehabilitation

- 97 — Medien, Kommunikation und Unterhaltungselektronik/
  Media, Communication and Entertainment Electronics

- 99 — Verkehrsmittel und Sonderfahrzeuge/
  Transportation and Special Use Vehicles

- 103 — Büro und Objekt/
  Office and Public Space

- 105 — Wohnung/
  Living

- 115 — Haushalt, Küche und Bad/
  Household, Kitchen and Bathroom

- 133 — Public Design/
  Public Design

- 139 — Freizeit, Sport und Spiel/
  Leisure, Sport and Play

- 149 — Accessoires/
  Accessories

- 153 — Gesamt-Ranking: Top 20/
  Overall Ranking: Top 20

- 159 — Hall of Fame Hersteller/
  Hall of Fame Manufacturers

- 163 — Adressen Hersteller/
  Addresses Manufacturers

Über das Ranking:Design/
About Ranking:Design

Das Ranking:Design 2002/2003 wertet zum sechsten Mal die wichtigsten Design-Wettbewerbe Deutschlands aus. Die vorliegenden Ergebnisse sind nicht nur eine Auflistung oder Zusammenfassung dieser Auswertung, sondern sie stellen die für Deutschland repräsentative Rangfolge des qualitativen Engagements von Industrie-Designern und Herstellern dar.

In den Publikationen zum Ranking:Design lässt sich über die Jahre vergleichen, wer Design intensiv als strategischen Wirtschaftsfaktor eingesetzt hat und erfolgreich aus den Wettbewerben hervorgegangen ist. Die kontinuierliche Präsenz einzelner Teilnehmer zeigt, wie nützlich präzise Design-Strategien für dauerhaften wirtschaftlichen Erfolg sind – auch für junge Design-Teams und kleinere Hersteller.

Erstmals in diesem Buch veröffentlichen wir eine „Hall of Fame", in der Teilnahme und Punktezahl aller Industrie-Designer und Hersteller aus den bisherigen Ranking:Design Auswertungen dargestellt wird.

Im Ranking:Design finden Unternehmer die in ihrer Sparte richtungsweisenden Gestalter, Industrie-Designern weist die Publikation den Weg zu designorientierten Herstellern. Und schlussendlich zeigt sie dem Verbraucher eine Auswahl gestalterisch herausragender Produkte. Durch die Einteilung in zehn Produktgruppen werden die Ergebnisse vergleichbar – und das Ranking:Design lässt sich als übersichtliches Nachschlagewerk nutzen.

The Ranking:Design 2002/2003 is assessing for the sixth time the most important German design competitions. The present results are not only a listing or compilation of this assessment, but also demonstrate for Germany a representative ranking of the qualitative commitment of industrial designers and manufacturers.

In the publications on Ranking:Design, comparison can be made over the years as to who intensively employed design as strategic economic factor and has successfully become distinctive among the competitors. The continuous presence of individual contestants shows how useful precise design strategies are for lasting economic success are – also for young design teams and small manufacturers.

For the first time we present in this publication a „Hall of Fame" in which the participation and the score of all Inustrial Designers and Manufactures from all previous Ranking:Design analyses are listed.

In the Ranking:Design, companies find trend-setting designers in their fields, the publication shows industrial designers the route to design-oriented manufacturers. And finally it shows the consumer a selection of outstandingly designed products. As a result of the division into ten product groups, the results are comparable – and the Ranking-Design can be used as an uncomplicated reference work.

Die Methode/
The Method

Das Ranking:Design 2002/2003 für Industrie-Design basiert auf der Auswertung von 19 bundes- und landesweiten Design-Wettbewerben, die regelmäßig ausgeschrieben werden. Die Rangfolge der Designer und Hersteller ergibt sich aus den bei diesen Wettbewerben in der jeweils jüngsten Auslobung erzielten Preisen und Auszeichnungen für die einzelnen Produkte.
Für jedes ausgezeichnete Produkt ergibt sich die Produktpunktzahl aus der Multiplikation von Wettbewerbs- und Auszeichnungsfaktor (siehe Tabelle). Aus der Addition der Produktpunktzahlen errechnet sich die Gesamtpunktzahl.

The Ranking:Design 2002/2003 for Industrial-Design is based on the analysis of 19 design competitions that are regularly announced in Germany. The ranking of the designers and manufacturers results from the prizes and awards achieved for individual products in the most recent rewards of these competitions.
For each product awarded a prize, the product points are calculated as the mathematical product of competition and award factors (see table). The sum of all product points denotes the overall points.

	Wettbewerbsfaktor/ Competition factor				
Bundespreis Produktdesign	10	Preis/ Prize	Anerkennung/ Recognition	–	–
reddot award product design	8	Best of the Best/ Best of the best	–	Auszeichnung/ Award	–
if Product Design Award		Top Ten/ Top ten	Bester der Kategorie/ Best of category	Auszeichnung/ Award	–
Busse Longlife Design Award	7	1. Preis/ 1st prize	2. Preis/ 2nd prize	3. Preis/ 3rd prize	Auszeichnung/ Award
Designpreis Brandenburg		1. Preis/ 1st prize	2. Preis/ 2nd prize	3. Preis/ 3rd prize	Anerkennung/ Recognition
Designpreis Mecklenburg-Vorpommern für Produktdesign		Preisträger/ Laureate	–	–	Anerkennung/ Recognition
Designpreis Rheinland-Pfalz Produktdesign		Preisträger/ Laureate	–	–	Anerkennung/ Recognition
Designpreis Schleswig-Holstein		Auszeichnung/ Award	–	–	Anerkennung/ Recognition
Internationaler Designpreis Baden-Württemberg	6	Preisträger/ Laureate	–	–	Auszeichnung/ Award
hamburgerdesignpreis		Auszeichnung/ Award	–	–	–
Saarländischer Staatspreis Produktdesign		Preisträger/ Laureate	–	–	–
Sächsischer Staatspreis für Design		Preisträger/ Laureate	–	–	–
Designpreis des Landes Nordrhein-Westfalen		Ehrenpreis/ Prize	–	–	–
Designpreis Thüringen		Preisträger/ Laureate	–	–	Auszeichnung/ Award
Design Plus Ambiente		Auszeichnung/ Award	–	–	–
Design Plus Paperworld		Auszeichnung/ Award	–	–	–
Design Plus ISH	4	Auszeichnung/ Award	–	–	–
DDC Designer bewerten Designer		Gold/ Gold	Silber/ Silver	Bronze/ Bronze	Finalist/ Finalist
Produkte des Jahres		Auszeichnung/ Award	–	–	–
		10	**9**	**8**	**7**	Auszeichnungsfaktor/ Award factor

Vorwort

Dr. Rainer Zimmermann
CEO BBDO Group Germany

Werbung vs. Design

Noch nie hat eine Gesellschaft so viele Artefakte erzeugt wie die unsere. Waren und Produkte sind ein wichtiger Bereich unseres symbolischen Universums geworden. Was und wie wir produzieren und konsumieren ist kultureller Ausdruck unseres Lebens: um auszudrücken, wer wir sind und wer wir nicht sind. In unserer Kommunikationsgesellschaft werden stark individualisierte Produkte, die über einen hohen kommunikativen und symbolischen Zeichenreichtum verfügen, immer wichtiger. Die Oberfläche dieser Güter, quasi das ästhetische und kommunikative Interface zum Konsumenten, muss künftig noch komplexer und flexibler werden, denn sie ist der Träger der zeichenhaften Vermittlung von Bedeutung und Botschaften.

Aus der Sicht der integrierten Kommunikation und Werbung wird häufig die eigene Rolle überschätzt und die Rolle des Designs unterschätzt. Viele Werber und Kommunikationsstrategen glauben noch heute, dass sie es sind, die den Dingen ihre Bedeutung einhauchen, doch in Wahrheit ist es die Industrie, die längst zum zentralen Symbolproduzenten geworden ist.

Bereits die Entscheidung für die Herstellung eines Produkts, das seinen Ort in einer bereits existierenden Produktwelt finden muss, ist ein kulturelles Statement und zugleich Antizipation von Bedeutungen, die bereits zirkulieren. Man muss deshalb die Bedeutungen in der Welt der Dinge und Zeichen kennen, um gutes Design zu machen.

Design gelingt dann, wenn der Vielfalt der symbolischen Formen eine neue hinzugefügt werden konnte.

Werbung und Kommunikation kann daher bestehende Bedeutungen des bereits fertigen und designten Produkts nur pointieren. Und nicht selten reicht es kaum zu mehr als der Bekanntmachung, dass es dieses Produkt nun gibt, damit die Konsumenten es ihrer meist enzyklopädischen Warenkenntnis hinzufügen können. Andererseits kann gute Kommunikation dem Konsumenten dabei helfen, die Form des Produkts zu verstehen und für sich selbst eine Bedeutung herzustellen. Denn Interpretation bedeutet Anstrengung, sie ist produktive Arbeit, wie es Umberto Eco ausgedrückt hat.

Aus Sicht des größten deutschen Kommunikations- und Werbekonzerns, zu dem zwei der erfolgreichsten Designer dieses Landes gehören (Peter Schmidt und Claus Koch), kann man den Entscheidern in der Industrie und den Experten in Werbung und kommerzieller Kommunikation nur empfehlen, sich von den Designern inspirieren zu lassen und ihr Wissen über die Gestaltung von Symbolen und Zeichen auch für die eigene Arbeit zu nutzen. Je mehr wir über den Prozess der Produktion und des Designs von Bedeutung lernen und über die Vielfalt des alltäglichen Gebrauchs und der kulturellen Kontexte wissen, desto präziser und kreativer können wir das Endprodukt im Schaufenster der Aufmerksamkeit inszenieren.

Preface

Dr. Rainer Zimmermann
CEO BBDO Group Germany

Advertising vs. Design

Never before has a society created so many artifacts as ours has. Products and goods have become an important part of our symbolic universe. How and what we produce and consume is a cultural expression of our lives: to express who we are and who we are not. Highly individualized products that are rich in communicative and figurative symbols are becoming even more significant in our communication society. The façade of these goods, which is more or less the esthetic and communicative interface to the consumer, must soon become even more complex and flexible – because it is the carrier of symbol-based transmission of meaning and messages.

From the point of view of an integrated communication and advertising, our own role is often overestimated whereas that of design is underestimated. Many advertisers and information strategists still believe today that they are the ones that give things their meanings, when in reality it is the industry that has long ago become the main producer of symbolism.

Even the decision to manufacture a product that must find its position in an already existing product world is a cultural statement, and simultaneously an anticipation of significances already in circulation. One must therefore know the meanings in the world of things and symbols, in order to create a good design. A design is only successful when you manage to introduce a new symbolic form to the variety of existing ones.

Advertising and communication can therefore do no more than stress existent meanings of already finished and designed products. And they can rarely do more than to simply announce that the product now exists, so that the consumers may add it to their mind-encyclopedia of ware-awareness. On the other hand, good communication can help the consumer to understand the form of the product and to form his or her own meaning. Because interpretation demands effort and it is productive work, as Umberto Eco once expressed.

From the viewpoint of the biggest German communications and advertising concern, which happens to involve two of the most successful designers in Germany (Peter Schmidt and Claus Koch), one can only recommend that the decision-makers in industry and the experts in advertising and commercial communication should get some inspiration for their own work from the designers and utilize their knowledge about the creation of symbols and signs. The more we learn about the process of production and the design of meaning and the diversity of day-to-day usage and cultural contexts, the more precisely and creatively we can stage the final product in the shop window of attention.

Die 100 Besten / Industrie-Design
The Top 100 / Industrial Design

Handwerk und Industrie
Trade and Industry

Rang/*Rank*

Festo / D-Denkendorf / 967 Punkte/*Points*	1
Teams Design / D-Esslingen / 552 Punkte/*Points*	2
Heidelberger Druckmaschinen / D-Heidelberg / 456 Punkte/*Points*	3
Design Tech Jürgen R. Schmid / D-Ammerbuch / 440 Punkte/*Points*	4
designpraxis diener / D-Ulm / 384 Punkte/*Points*	5
MA Design / D-Kiel / 248 Punkte/*Points*	6
Ergonomi Design / S-Bromma / 216 Punkte/*Points*	7
Henssler und Schultheiss / D-Schwäbisch Gmünd / 192 Punkte/*Points*	8
Studiowerk Design / D-Inning / 192 Punkte/*Points*	8
BAHCO BELZER / D-Wuppertal / 144 Punkte/*Points*	10
Proform Design / D-Winnenden / 144 Punkte/*Points*	10

Handwerk und Industrie/*Trade and Industry*

Festo

Festo AG & Co. KG
Corporate Design

Anschrift/*Address*
Rechbergstraße 3
D-73770 Denkendorf
Ansprechpartner/*Contact*
Prof. Dipl.-Ing. Axel Thallemer
Head of Corporate Design
Telefon/*Phone*
+49(0)711/3 47 38 80
Telefax/*Fax*
+49(0)711/3 47 38 99
E-mail/*E-mail*
tem@festo.com

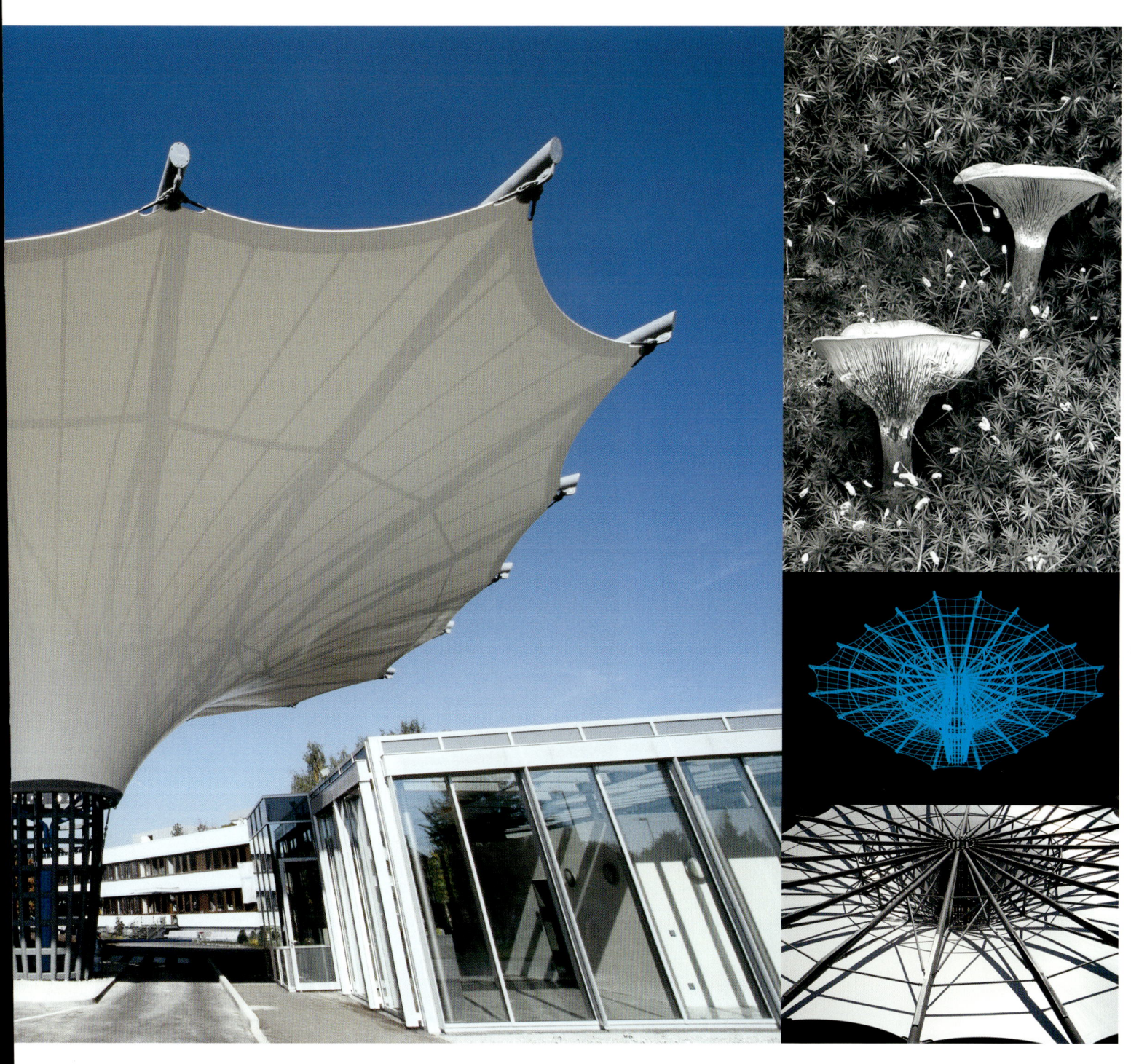

Handwerk und Industrie / Trade and Industry

Festo 1

Teams Design

Anschrift/*Address*
Kollwitzstraße 1
D-73728 Esslingen

Geschäftsführung/*Management*
Reinhard Renner
Hans Peter Aglassinger
Klaus Baumgartner

Telefon/*Phone*
+49 (0)711/35 17 65-0

Telefax/*Fax*
+49 (0)711/35 17 65-25

E-mail/*E-mail*
info@teams-design.de

Internet/*Website*
www.teamsdesign.de

Gründungsdatum/*Foundation*
1956 als Slany Design durch
Prof. H.E. Slany
1987 Verbreiterung der
Aktionsbasis durch Aufnahme
von R. Renner und K. Schön in
die Geschäftsführung
1998 Gründung von Teams Design,
USA, mit Sitz in Chicago
2002 Gründung von Teams Design,
Hamburg
1956 as Slany Design by
Prof. H.E. Slany
1987 Expansion of the leadership
by appointing R. Renner and
K. Schön to the board
1998 Founding of Teams Design,
USA in Chicago
2002 Founding of Teams Design,
Hamburg

Mitarbeiter/*Employees*
34

Ausstattung/*Equipment*
CAD, Modellbau, DTP
CAD, model making, DTP

Firmenphilosophie

Seit über 40 Jahren werden wir mit der Gestaltung von industriell gefertigten Produkten beauftragt und gehören zu den erfahrensten und profiliertesten Design-Teams. Mit 34 Mitarbeitern zählen wir zu den größten Designagenturen. Das Team ist international besetzt. Unser Team hat bisher annähernd 1000 nationale und internationale Designauszeichnungen für realisierte Produkte erhalten – verliehen von internationalen Jurys. Das ist weltweit einmalig.
Viele von uns gestaltete Produkte erhielten Auszeichnungen für Langzeit-Design.
1990 Design Team des Jahres (Design Zentrum Nordrhein Westfalen)
1996 Platz 2 der Gesamtwertung im Ranking Top Ten International (Design Zentrum Nordrhein Westfalen)
1997 Ranking:Design (d…c Unternehmensberatung) Platz 2 im Gesamtranking. Platz 1 in der Kategorie Handwerk und Industrie.
In 3 weiteren Kategorien jeweils unter den ersten 10.
1998/99 Platz 1 in der Kategorie Handwerk und Industrie (Ranking:Design)
1999 Designpreis des Jahrzehnts von Business Week und IDSA

Referenzen

Einmalig ist, dass die Mehrzahl unserer Kunden seit vielen Jahrzehnten mit uns zusammenarbeitet. Auf den Gebieten Investitionsgüter und Konsumgüter sind wir für Konzerne und mittelständische Unternehmen tätig, die auf ihren Gebieten in der Regel Marktführer sind.
Zum Beispiel: Bosch (seit 1957), Leifheit (seit 1959), Silit (seit 1962), Kärcher (seit 1964), Leitz (seit 1973), Still (seit 1987), Weishaupt (seit 1987), Wolfcraft (seit 1997).

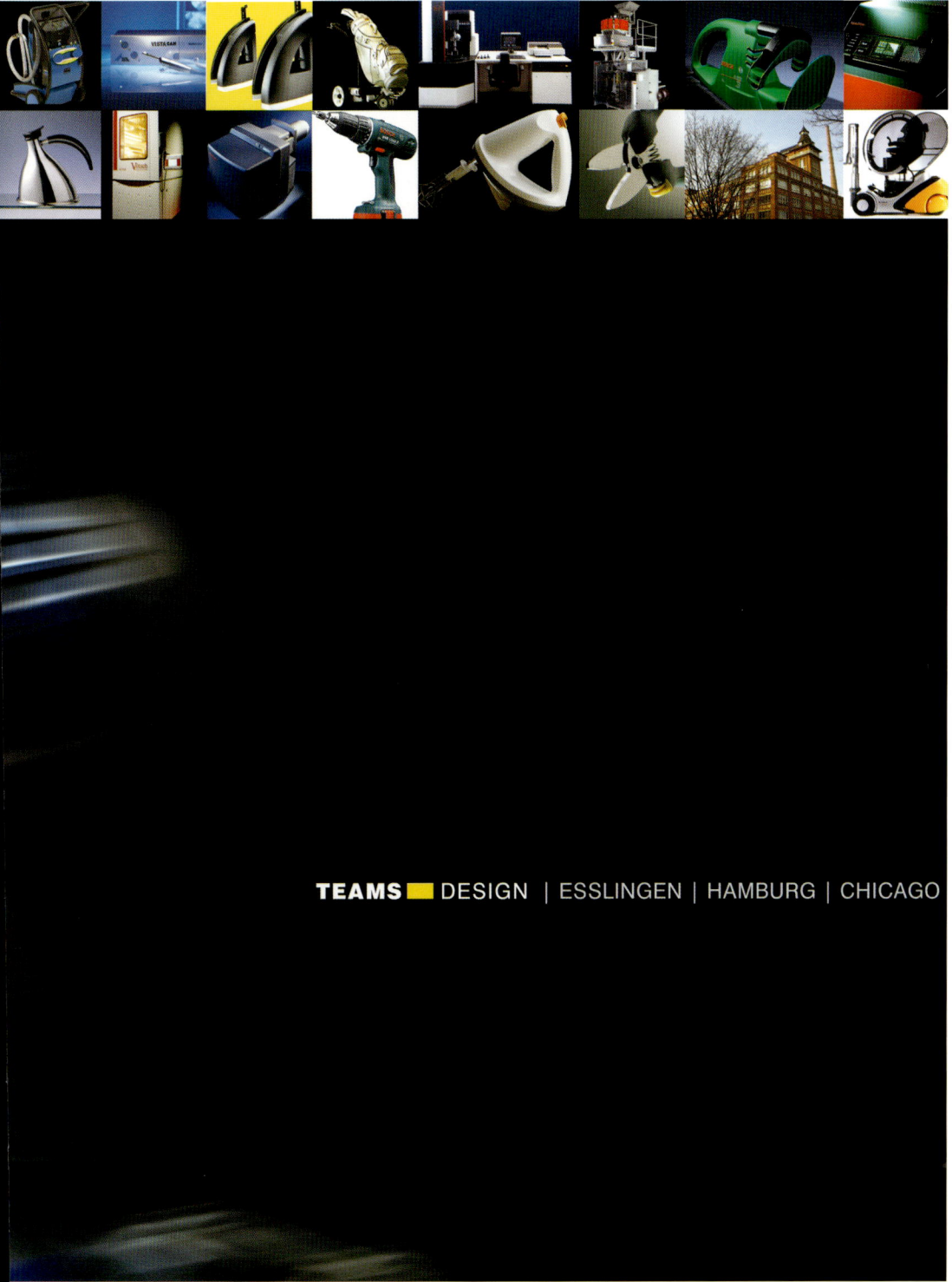

TEAMS DESIGN | ESSLINGEN | HAMBURG | CHICAGO

Corporate Philosophy
For over 40 years we have been receiving commissions for the design of industrially produced goods and are among the most experienced and distinguished design agencies. The Team consists of an international staff.
Our Team has thus far received almost 1000 national and international design awards for realized products – awarded by international juries. Many products designed by us have received awards for longterm design.
1990 Design Team of the Year (Design Center Northrhine Westphalia)
1996 2nd place in the Ranking Top Ten International (Design Center Northrhine Westphalia)
1997 Ranking:Design (d...c brand + design consultants) rank 2 in the overall ranking. Rank 1 in the trade and industry category, among the top ten in 3 other categories.
1998 1st place in the trade and industry category (Ranking:Design)
1999 Design of the decades award (Business Week and IDSA).

References
What's unique is that most of our clients have been working with us for decades. We are working for large cooperations and medium-sized enterprises who generally are market leaders in their industries in the fields of investment goods and consumer goods. For example: Bosch (since 1957), Leifheit (since 1959), Silit (since 1962), Kärcher (since 1964), Leitz (since 1973), Still (since 1987), Weishaupt (since 1987), Wolfcraft (since 1997).

Medizin und Rehabilitation
Medicine and Rehabilitation

	Rang/*Rank*
Held + Team / D-Hamburg / 336 Punkte/*Points*	1
designafairs / D-München / 328 Punkte/*Points*	2
piu products / D-Essen / 256 Punkte/*Points*	3
Rokitta Produkt & Markenästhetik / D-Hamburg / 214 Punkte/*Points*	4
einmaleins - Büro für Gestaltung / D-Burgrieden / 170 Punkte/*Points*	5
Ganymed / D-Berg / 132 Punkte/*Points*	6
Ergonomi Design / S-Bromma / 128 Punkte/*Points*	7
Kienzledesign / D-Konstanz / 128 Punkte/*Points*	7
Rainer Schindhelm / D-Rotthalmünster / 124 Punkte/*Points*	9
Pilotprojekt / D-Münster / 100 Punkte/*Points*	10

Held+Team

Anschrift/*Address*
Schrammsweg 11
D-20249 Hamburg
Ansprechpartner/*Contact*
Fred Held
Telefon/*Phone*
+49 (0)40/48 07 075
Telefax/*Fax*
+49 (0)40/48 07 076
E-mail/*E-mail*
Held.u.Team@t-online.de
Internet/*Website*
www.HeldundTeam.de
Gründungsdatum/*Foundation*
7/97
Referenzen/*References*
Tätig für über 30 Unternehmen
Operating for more than 30 enterprises
Tätigkeitsfelder/*Fields of Activity*
Spezialisiert auf die Entwicklung medizintechnischer Produkte mit denen über 90 % des Honorarumsatzes erzielt werden (Designentwicklung 55 %, Ergonomieentwicklung 25 %, Innovation/Ideenentwicklung 15 %, Gebrauchsanweisungen 5 %).
Specialized in the development of medical technology products, more than 90 % of the turnover (design development 55 %, ergonomics development 25 %, innovation/finding ideas 15 %, instruction manuals 5 %).

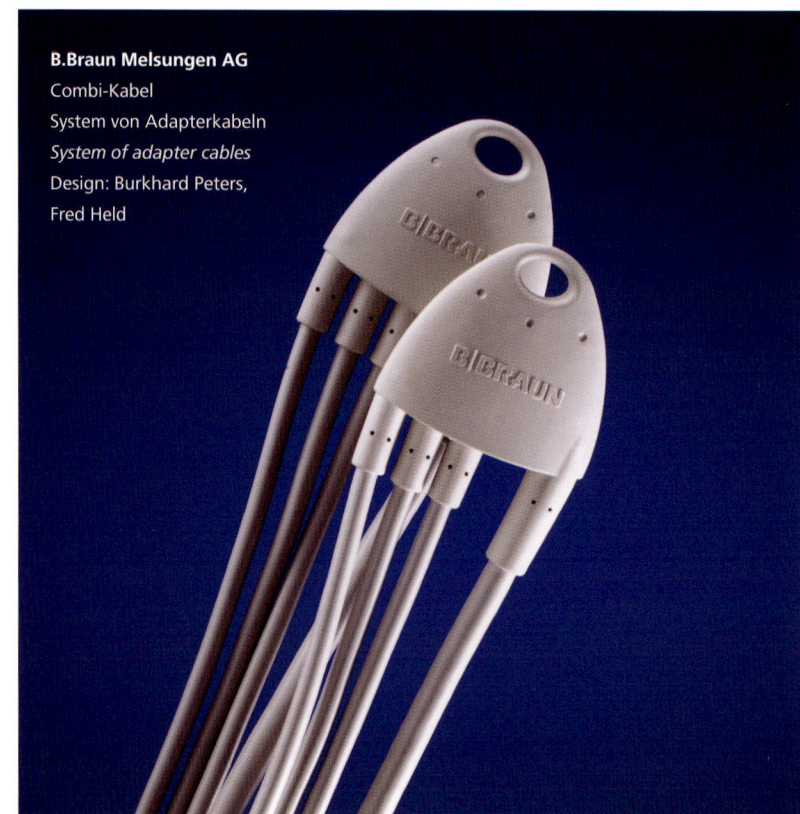

B.Braun Melsungen AG
Combi-Kabel
System von Adapterkabeln
System of adapter cables
Design: Burkhard Peters,
Fred Held

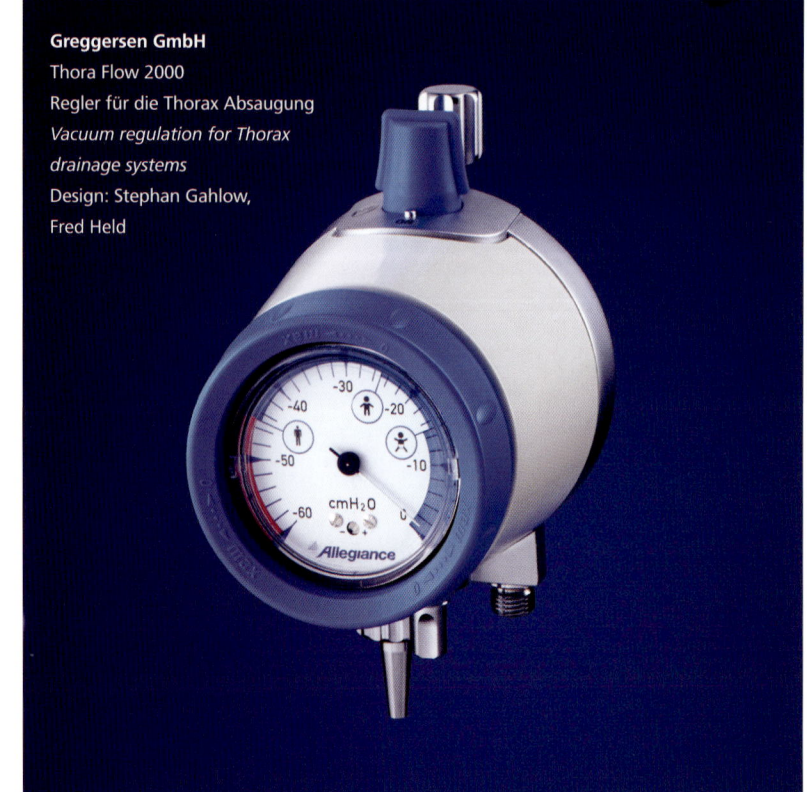

Greggersen GmbH
Thora Flow 2000
Regler für die Thorax Absaugung
Vacuum regulation for Thorax drainage systems
Design: Stephan Gahlow,
Fred Held

Bowa electronic GmbH
Elektrodenhandgriff
mit Rauchabsaugung
*Electrode hand grip
with optional smoke suction*
Design: Fred Held

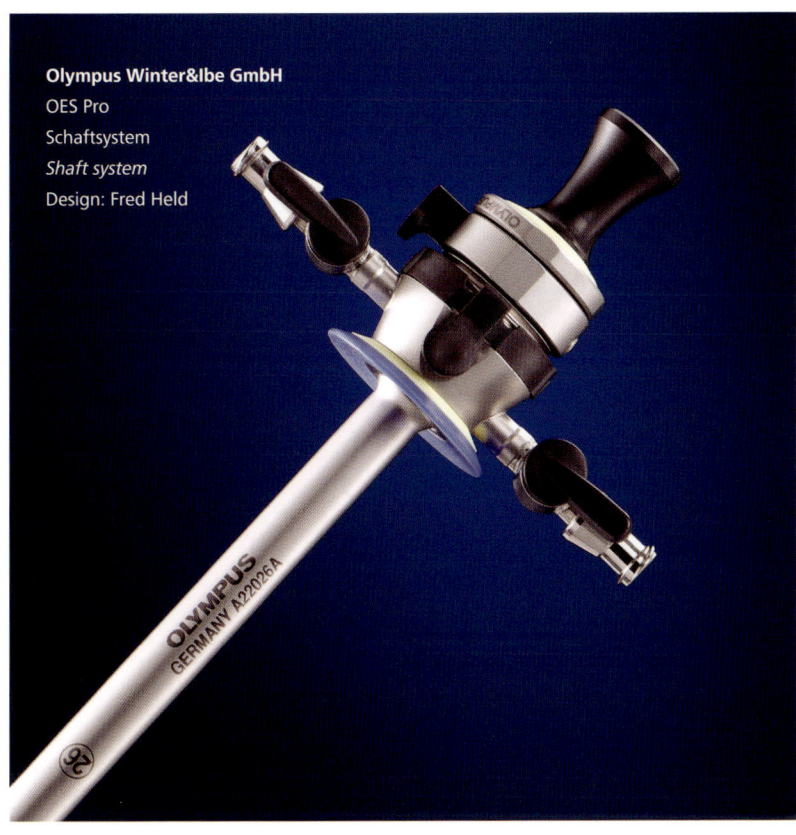

Olympus Winter&Ibe GmbH
OES Pro
Schaftsystem
Shaft system
Design: Fred Held

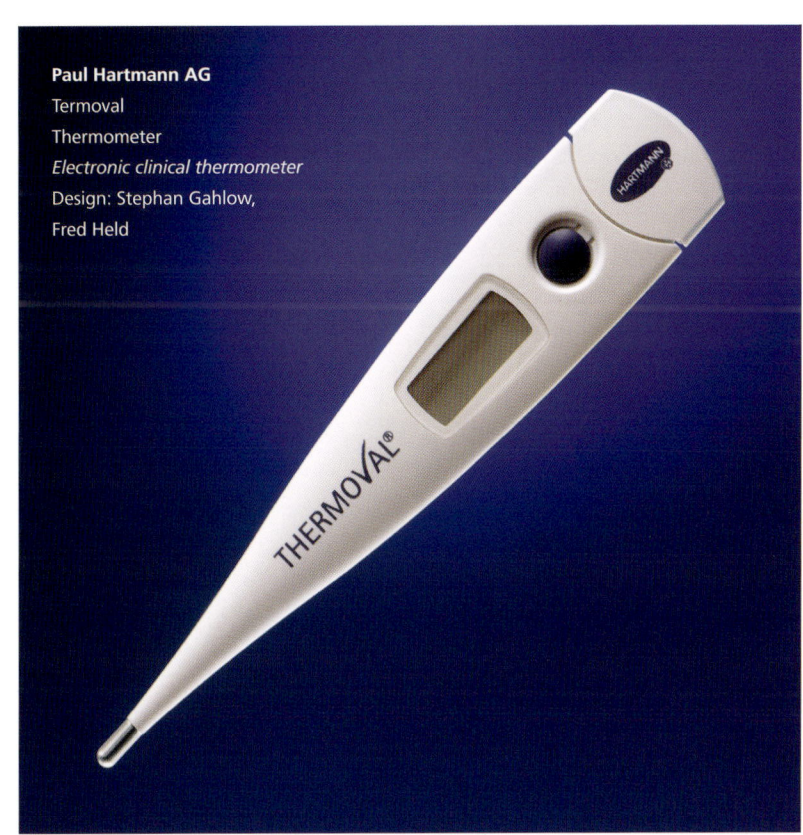

Paul Hartmann AG
Termoval
Thermometer
Electronic clinical thermometer
Design: Stephan Gahlow,
Fred Held

Ganymed GmbH

Anschrift/*Address*
Breitenloh 7
D-82335 Berg

Ansprechpartner/*Contact*
Karen Ostertag
Dr. Sigmar Klose

Design/*Design*
Karen Ostertag

Telefon/*Phone*
+49 (0)8151/95 32 35

Telefax/*Fax*
+49 (0)8151/95 32 56

E-mail/*E-mail*
info@ganymed.biz

Internet/*Website*
www.ganymed.biz

Gründungsdatum/*Foundation*
1998

Tätigkeitsfelder/*Fields of Activity*
Mobilitätshilfen – Entwicklung, Fertigung und Vertrieb
Walking Aids – development, production and distribution

Seit mehr als 3.000 Jahren hat es keine Weiterentwicklung von Gehhilfen gegeben, sieht man davon ab, dass aus der Achselkrücke in fast allen Ländern die sogenannte Unterarmgehhilfe üblich geworden ist. Diese wird de facto unverändert seit dem 1. Weltkrieg hergestellt, wie allgemein bekannt.

Das GANYMED® Concept basiert auf der Vorstellung, all das zu vermeiden, was Betroffene bislang beklagen: es galt, eine Gehhilfe zu entwickeln, die nicht umfällt, weil man sie überall anhängen kann und damit unabhängig von Hilfe Dritter macht, die schmerzvermeidend wirkt durch physiologisch richtige Konstruktion und Materialwahl sowie den Patienten nicht gebrechlicher hält, als er es ist. Und nicht zuletzt eine Gehhilfe schafft, die durch ihren ästhetischen Anspruch die Würde des körperlich versehrten Menschen nicht beschädigt.

Die GANYMED® Gehhilfen wurden seit dem Jahr ihrer Markteinführung 1998 mehrfach ausgezeichnet für Innovation und Design.

Sie befinden sich in der Ständigen Sammlung der Moderne im Museum für Kunst und Gewerbe, Hamburg.

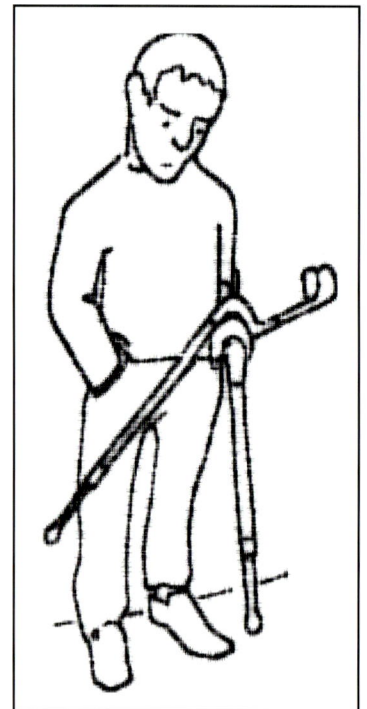
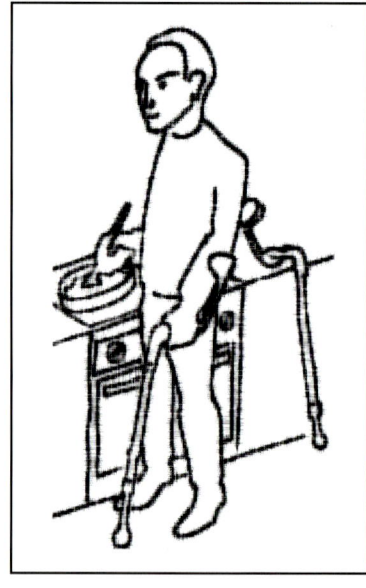

Die GANYMED® Gehhilfen
lassen sich überall anhängen und vermeiden die bekannten Beschwerden von Patienten mit herkömmlichen Produkten.

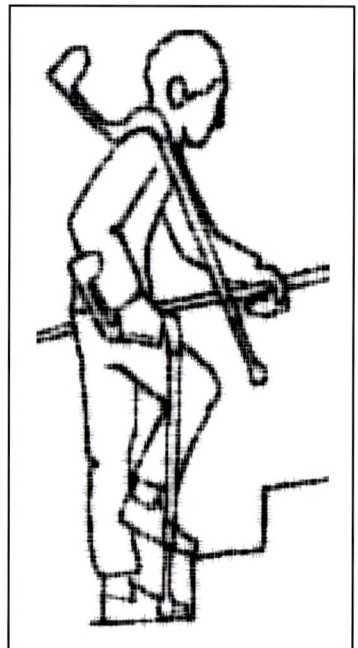

The GANYMED® crutches
can be hung anywhere; they avoid the well known pains of patients caused by conventional products.

There has been no real improvement of walking aids since more than 3,000 years except the shoulder sprag is replaced by the lower arm going support in almost all countries. The latter is manufactured for the last 100 years almost without change.

The GANYMED® Concept is based on the principle to avoid all complaints the suffering patients had until now: to avoid falling down of the crutches, because it can be hung on many places, assistance of other people is no longer necessary; to avoid pain by optimized design and choice of material. Many of the patients need not appear sick and humble.

The GANYMED® walking aids have been awarded for innovation and design on numerous occasions since their market introduction in 1998.

They are shown in the Permanent Exhibition of Modernity in Museum of Art and Handicraft, Hamburg.

Medien, Kommunikation und Unterhaltungselektronik
Media, Communication and Entertainment Electronics

	Rang/*Rank*
IBM / D-Herrenberg / 1424 Punkte/*Points*	1
Sony Europe / D-Berlin / 1376 Punkte/*Points*	2
Samsung Electronics / D-Schwalbach / 712 Punkte/*Points*	3
Canon / D-Krefeld / 512 Punkte/*Points*	4
Apple Computer / D-Feldkirchen / 400 Punkte/*Points*	5
Phoenix Product Design / D-Stuttgart / 398 Punkte/*Points*	6
MA Design / D-Kiel / 358 Punkte/*Points*	7
Microsoft / D-Unterschleißheim / 320 Punkte/*Points*	8
designafairs / D-München / 298 Punkte/*Points*	9
Fitch / USA-Worthington / 256 Punkte/*Points*	10
Philips Design / NL-Eindhoven / 256 Punkte/*Points*	10

Verkehrsmittel und Sonderfahrzeuge
Transportation and Special Use Vehicles

Rang/*Rank*

BMW / D-München / 548 Punkte/*Points*	1
Neumeister Design / D-München / 308 Punkte/*Points*	2
Crown Gabelstapler / D-München / 256 Punkte/*Points*	3
Dr. Ing. h.c. F. Porsche / D-Stuttgart / 256 Punkte/*Points*	3
Deutsche Bahn / D-Berlin / 228 Punkte/*Points*	5
DaimlerChrysler / D-Sindelfingen / 206 Punkte/*Points*	6
Audi / D-Ingolstadt / 178 Punkte/*Points*	7
Designworks/USA / D-München / 164 Punkte/*Points*	8
Honda / D-Offenbach / 144 Punkte/*Points*	9
Jaguar / D-Kronberg / 144 Punkte/*Points*	9

Das Design der BMW Group bezieht seine Authentizität aus der Unternehmenstradition und ist gleichzeitig wegweisend und nachhaltig. Tradition und Zukunftsorientierung prägen die einzigartige Designkultur der BMW Group.

The design of the BMW Group takes its authenticity from the company's tradition and is pioneering and enduring.
Tradition and future orientation characterize the unique design culture of the BMW Group.

BMW AG

Anschrift/*Address*
D-80788 München
Ansprechpartner/*Contact*
Abteilung Öffentlichkeitsarbeit
Public Relation Department
Telefon/*Phone*
+49 (0)89/38 20
Internet/*Website*
www.BMWgroup.de

Der Z8 als Träger zukunftsweisender Technologien nimmt mit seiner organischen Gestalt traditionelle Roadsterelemente auf und interpretiert diese auf BMW typische, spannungsvolle Weise neu.
Die außergewöhnliche Interieurgestaltung lässt die Insassen „Freude am Fahren" pur erleben.
With its organic form the Z8 embodies trend-setting technologies and traditional roadster elements and interprets these in a new tensionful way as a typical BMW.
Emphasized by the extraordinary interior design the passengers can feel „the ultimate driving experience".

Crown zählt zu den weltweit führenden Herstellern von Elektro-Flurförderzeugen. Seit über 40 Jahren setzen Crown Produkte Industriestandards in Design, Ergonomie und Innovation.

Das Crown Design Center ist heute ein strategischer Part der Produktentwicklung mit der Aufgabe, den Nutzen für den Kunden zu schaffen. Das Team ist im Produktentwicklungsprozess von Anfang an involviert - Forschung, Konzepterstellung, Bau von 1:1 Modellen, CAD und Feldtests. Ausführliche Forschung bei Anwendern und ein straff organisierter Entwicklungsprozess sind wichtige Schlüsselfaktoren, die zur Produktinnovation und Optimierung des Nutzens für den Kunden beitragen.

Crown Produkte sind weltweit bekannt für ihren hohen Interaktionswert, Designqualität und technologischen Fortschritt.

Crown Gabelstapler GmbH

Anschrift/*Address*
Moosacher Straße 52
D-80809 München

Ansprechpartner/*Contact*
Jim Kraimer

Telefon/*Phone*
+49 (0)89/93 002-105

Telefax/*Fax*
+49 (0)89/93 002-302

E-mail/*E-mail*
jim.kraimer@crown.com

Internet/*Website*
www.crown.com

Gründungsdatum/*Foundation*
1945

Mitarbeiter/*Employees*
6.500 weltweit, 1.100 in Europa (18 in Design Center/Design Center Europe)
6,500 worldwide, 1,100 in Europe (18 in Design Center/Design Center Europe)

Filialen/*Branch Offices*
Sitz in New Bremen, Ohio, USA (Design Center), Europazentrale in München (Design Center Europe) 10 Produktionsstandorte weltweit (USA, Mexiko, Deutschland, Irland, Australien), 63 Niederlassungen weltweit, 12 in Europa
World Headquarter in New Bremen, Ohio, USA (location of Design Center), European Headquarter in Munich, Germany (location of Design Center Europe), 10 manufacturing sites worldwide (USA, Mexico, Germany, Ireland, Australia), 63 sales branches worldwide, 12 in Europe

Umsatz/*Turnover*
1,096 Milliarden Euro (2001)
1.096 Billion Euro (2001)

Kunden/*Clients*
Warenlager, Distributionszentren, Fabriken, Einzelhandel
Warehouses, distribution centers, factories, and retail stores

Tätigkeitsfelder/*Fields of Activity*
Design, Entwicklung, Produktion und Distribution einer breiten Produktpalette von elektromotorisch angetriebenen Flurförderzeugen. Die Produktpalette reicht vom Hand-Gabelhubwagen, Geh-Gabelhochhubwagen, Niederhubkommissionierer, Schlepper, Gegengewichtsstapler, Schubmaststapler, Kommissionierer bis hin zum Hochregalstapler und Multifunktionsgerät.
Design, development, manufacturing, and distribution of a wide range of electric powered material handling equipment. Products include pedestrian and rider pallet trucks, stackers, tow tractors, counterbalanced trucks, reach trucks, stockpickers, turret trucks, and work-assist products.

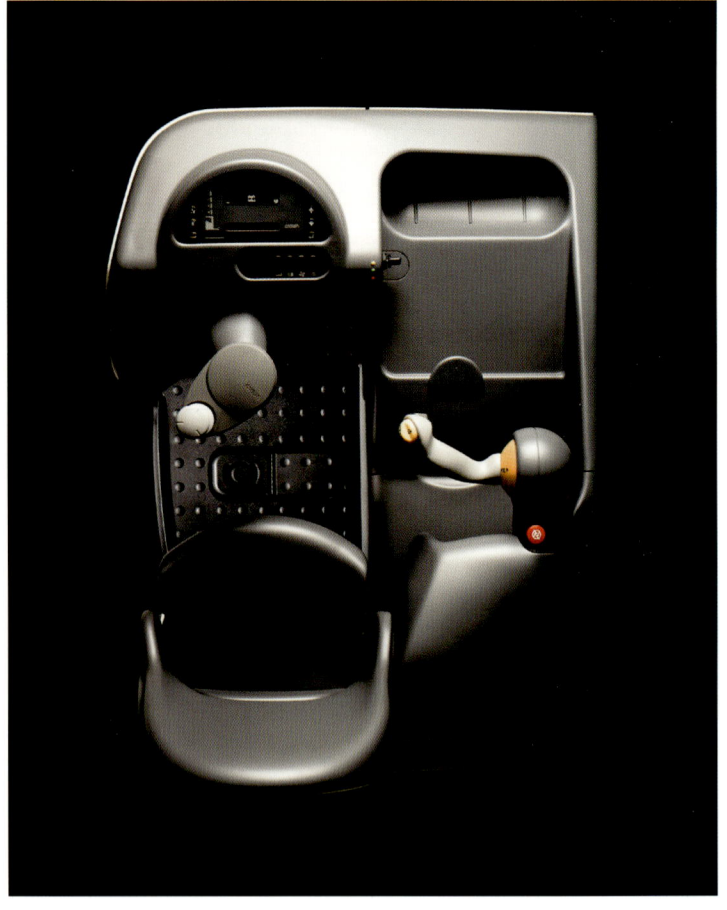

Serie RR 5200 S
Die Bedienerzentrale erlaubt dem Fahrer maximale Kontrolle, Flexibilität und Produktivität durch innovative Sitz/Lehn/Standposition und verstellbare Kontrollhebel.
RR 5200S Series
The Work Relief Center maximizes operator control, flexibility and productivity with innovative sit/lean/stand positioning and fully adjustable controls.

Serie FC 4000
Durch das innovative Design hat der Fahrer eine ausgezeichnete Sicht nach vorne und einen bequemen Ein- und Ausstieg.
FC 4000 Series
The innovative Operator Forward design creates excellent forward visibility and easy on/off access.

Serie WP 2000
Der Geh-Gabelhubwagen WP 2000 ist bedienerfreundlich, robust und auch bei engen Platzverhältnissen sehr manövrierfähig.
WP 2000 Series
The WP 2000 pallet truck is recognized for being user-friendly, robust and highly maneuverable in tight spaces.

Crown Equipment Corporation is one of the leading manufacturers of material handling equipment in the world. For over 40 years Crown products have set industry standards in design, ergonomics, and innovation.

Today the Corporate Design Center is a strategic part of product development with the mission of creating value for the customer. The team is involved throughout the entire product development process, including research, concept development, construction of mockups, CAD, and field testing. Intensive user research and a rigorous development process have been key factors in creating customer value and product innovation that have driven the company to success.

Crown products are recognized around the world for their superior operator interface, design quality, and technology advances.

Serie RR 5200
Der Multi-Funktions-Hebel vereint Ergonomie und Funktionalität, um Fahren, Heben und Ein- und Auslagern schnell und bequem durchzuführen.
RR 5200 Series
The Multi-Task Control combines ergonomics and functionality to allow easy blending of travel, lift and reach functions.

Büro und Objekt
Office and Public Space

Rang/*Rank*

SPECTRAL GESELLSCHAFT FÜR LICHTTECHNIK / D-Freiburg / 336 Punkte/*Points*	1
wiege Entwicklungsges. / D-Bad Münder / 320 Punkte/*Points*	2
designafairs / D-München / 256 Punkte/*Points*	3
Foster and Partners / GB-London / 232 Punkte/*Points*	4
Jehs & Laub / D-Stuttgart / 192 Punkte/*Points*	5
Justus Kolberg, Office for Industrial Design / D-Hamburg / 192 Punkte/*Points*	5
Sedus Stoll / D-Waldshut / 192 Punkte/*Points*	5
Carsten Gollnick product design/interior design / D-Berlin / 184 Punkte/*Points*	8
Peter Maly / D-Hamburg / 184 Punkte/*Points*	8
James Irvine / I-Mailand / 144 Punkte/*Points*	10
Korb + Korb / CH-Baden / 144 Punkte/*Points*	10
Erik Magnussen / DK-Klampenborg / 144 Punkte/*Points*	10
Designstudio Matteo Thun / I-Mailand / 144 Punkte/*Points*	10

Wohnung
Living

	Rang/*Rank*
Phoenix Product Design / D-Stuttgart / 444 Punkte/*Points*	1
nya nordiska / D-Dannenberg / 256 Punkte/*Points*	2
Matthias Bader / D-Landau / 148 Punkte/*Points*	3
Grimshaw Industrial Design / GB-London / 128 Punkte/*Points*	4
Peter Maly / D-Hamburg / 128 Punkte/*Points*	4
Pascal Mourgue / F-Montreuil-Sous-Bois / 128 Punkte/*Points*	4
Phanos Gestaltung + Vertrieb / D-Bremen / 128 Punkte/*Points*	4
arche design H. Piltz / D-Münster / 128 Punkte/*Points*	4
Sieger Design / D-Sassenberg / 128 Punkte/*Points*	4
OLIGO Lichttechnik / D-St. Augustin / 124 Punkte/*Points*	10

nya nordiska

Anschrift/*Address*
An den Ratswiesen
D-29451 Dannenberg

Ansprechpartner/*Contact*
Bernhard Hansl

Telefon/*Phone*
+49 (0)5861/809-43

Telefax/*Fax*
+49 (0)5861/809-12

E-mail/*E-mail*
nya@nya.com

Internet/*Website*
www.nya.com

Gründungsdatum/*Foundation*
1964

Mitarbeiter/*Employees*
circa 100

Filiale/*Branch Office*
Como, Paris, London, Tokio

Tätigkeitsfelder/*Fields of Activity*
Produktentwicklung und Vertrieb von Heimtextilien
Product development and distribution of home textiles

BACCARA

Flor-Gewebe auf reinseidener Kette, Flor geschnitten und im Finish auf „Strich" gebracht und zu guter Letzt mit goldener Pigment-Paste bedruckt. Das ist es. Punkt.

Wo bleibt der Schmelz der Naturseide, das Schmeicheln der seidigen Glanz-Viskose, die Aura dieser traumhaften Farbigkeit und die Einfühlsamkeit der Dessinierung, und wo bleibt der Mattschimmer des Goldes und der unglaubliche Lüster des Samt-Velours?
Ist das eine Frage?

Piled fabric on a pure silk weft. The pile cut and brushed to a raised nap and then finished with a golden pigment paste print. That's all there is to it. Full stop.

What happened to the bloom of natural silk, the smoothness of silky viscose. The aura given by the color-richness and the glowing warmth of the design? And what of the pale glimmer of gold, the incredible luster of velvet? Why are you asking?

DOVELLI

Zwei Gewebe zu einem vereint, sozusagen ein Doppelgewebe?

So einfach ist das nicht: Das Gewebe ist nur partiell doppelt und bildet Streifen - die farbig, auch noch verschieden farbig sind und es lässt das eine Gewebe wie es ist - nämlich einfach - und es bleibt dadurch - im Gegensatz zu den doppelten Partien - transparent.

Two fabrics made into one, as it were a double fabric ?

It is not really that simple: The fabrics are only partially put together and this method forms stripes in different colors, but leaves the material as it is - simple - and that is how it stays - except for the doubled parts - transparent.

MATAKHA
Hier wird Edles mit Edlem gemischt: reine Seide mit feinster Wolle,
aufgefangen im puristischen Streifendessin. Ein Scherli mit Extraklasse.

*Here noblesse is mixed with noblesse: pure silk with finest wool,
captured in a puristic stripe design. A Scherli with extra class.*

Wohnung/Living

Oligo

10

OLIGO Lichttechnik GmbH

Anschrift/Address
Firmensitz/Head Office
Meysstraße 22-24
D-53773 Hennef/Sieg
Telefon/Phone
+49 (0)2242/87 02-0
Telefax/Fax
+49 (0)2242/87 02-88
E-Mail/E-Mail
info@oligo.de
Internet/Website
www.oligo.de
Geschäftsführung/
Managing director
Ralf Keferstein
Marketingabteilung/
Marketing Department
Schloßstraße 7
D-53757 Sankt Augustin
Telefon/Phone
+49 (0)2241/2 34 17-3
Telefax/Fax
+49 (0)2241/2 34 17-44
Ansprechpartner/Contact
Dipl.-Des. Klaus Liese
E-Mail/E-Mail
klaus.liese@oligo.de
Gründungsdatum/Foundation
1987
Mitarbeiterzahl/Employees
150
Kunden/Clients
Leuchtenfachhändler, Lichtplaner, Architekten
Light Specialists, Light Planners, Architects
Vertrieb/Sales department
Exclusivvertretungen in über 30 Ländern
Exclusive representation in 30 countries
Tätigkeitsfelder/Fields of Activity
Herstellung und Vertrieb moderner Leuchten für den Wohn- und Geschäftsbereich
The manufacture and sales of modern lamps for domestic and business areas
Auszeichnungen/Awards
iF - Design Award 1997
Red dot award 1997, 1998, 2001
Ehrenpreis Produktdesign des Landes Nordrhein-Westfalen 2001
Nominiert für den Bundespreis Produktdesign 2002

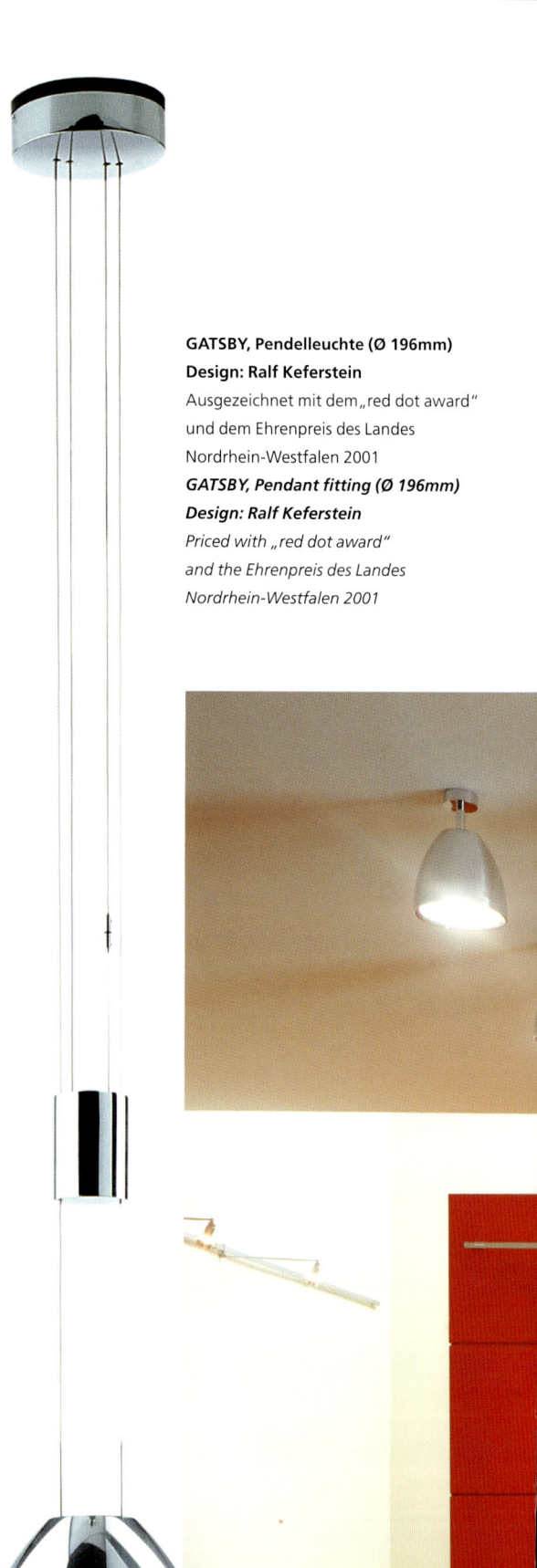

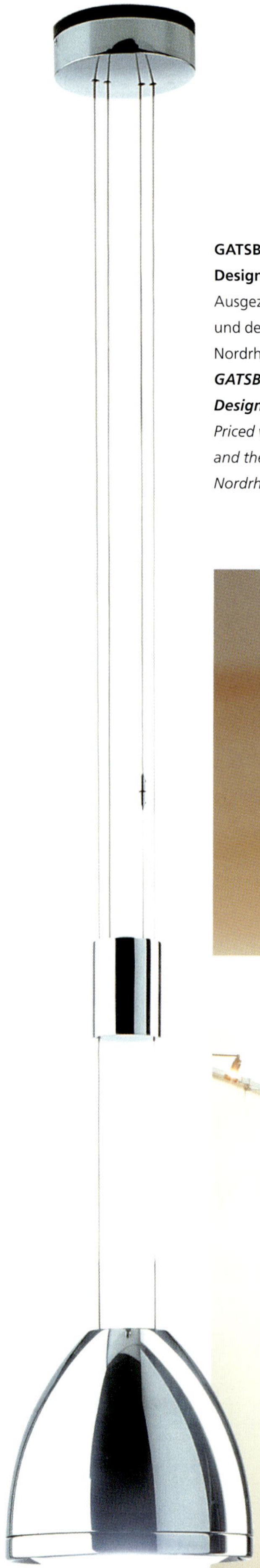

OLIGO
feel the light

OLIGO entwickelt, produziert und vermarktet weltweit hochwertige Leuchten und Lichtsysteme. Die innovative Verknüpfung von Design und Funktionalität sowie eine präzise Detailverarbeitung mit hohem Qualitätsanspruch kennzeichnen die Produkte und dokumentieren das Selbstverständnis der Unternehmenskultur. Eine Synthese aus funktioneller Sachlichkeit, zeitloser Formensprache und *feel the light*. Diesem Leitgedanken folgend hat sich das Unternehmen unter seinem Gründer Ralf Keferstein seit 1987 den Weg zu einem führenden europäischen Leuchtenhersteller bereitet. Mit dem Namen OLIGO verbindet der Markt insbesondere die formale Umsetzung von Emotion, Ästhetik und Funktion in unverwechselbare lichttechnische Produkte. Dabei ist der Entwicklungs- und Designprozess von einem gesamtheitlichen Denken geprägt.
Technische Innovation, Formensprache und Ergonomie der Produkte ordnen sich den Bedürfnissen seiner Benutzer unter. Alle Prozesse im Unternehmen, von der Entwicklung mit 3D-Animation und Konstruktion über die Produktionssteuerung und Vertriebsabwicklung, werden von modernster Computertechnik unterstützt.
Seit 2001 werden neben den modernen Wohnraumleuchten auch Leuchten und Lichtsysteme für den Shop- und Office Bereich hergestellt.
Damit folgt das Unternehmen den Bedürfnissen des Marktes nach einem umfassenden Angebot.

GATSBY, Pendelleuchte (Ø 196mm)
Design: Ralf Keferstein
Ausgezeichnet mit dem „red dot award" und dem Ehrenpreis des Landes Nordrhein-Westfalen 2001
GATSBY, Pendant fitting (Ø 196mm)
Design: Ralf Keferstein
Priced with „red dot award" and the Ehrenpreis des Landes Nordrhein-Westfalen 2001

CHECK-IN, 230V~ Stromschiene
mit Strahler GATE B SEVEN
CHECK-IN, 230V~ track
with spot light GATE B SEVEN

OLIGO
feel the light

OLIGO develop, manufacture and market world-wide high-quality lights and lighting systems. The products are characterised by an innovative combination of design, functionality and accurate handling of details with an insistence on the highest levels of quality. They provide concrete evidence of the company's philosophy.
A synthesis of functional simplicity, timeless design and feel the light.
Since 1987 the company has prepared the ground for becoming one of Europe's leading lighting manufacturers, through following this central principle under the guidance of its founder, Ralf Keferstein. The name of OLIGO is associated in the market in particular with the expression of emotion, aesthetics and function in the form of unmistakable lighting products. The development and design process is characterised by an integrating philosophy. The products' technical innovation, style and ergonomics are subsidiary to the needs of their users.
All the processes within the company, from development using 3D simulations, construction, through to production control and sales, are supported by the latest computer technology.
Since 2001, lamps and lighting systems for retail and office areas have been manufactured in addition to modern domestic lamps. In this way, the company is offering a comprehensive range to meet the needs of the market.

Haushalt, Küche und Bad
Household, Kitchen and Bath

	Rang/*Rank*
Siemens-Electrogeräte / D-München / 896 Punkte/*Points*	1
Phoenix Product Design / D-Stuttgart / 890 Punkte/*Points*	2
Studio Ambrozus / D-Köln / 464 Punkte/*Points*	3
Robert Bosch Hausgeräte / D-München / 362 Punkte/*Points*	4
Teams Design / D-Esslingen / 360 Punkte/*Points*	5
AEG Hausgeräte / D-Nürnberg / 192 Punkte/*Points*	6
Miele & Cie. / D-Gütersloh / 192 Punkte/*Points*	6
Studio X / GB-London / 192 Punkte/*Points*	6
Tools Design / DK-Kopenhagen / 192 Punkte/*Points*	6
Heidebrecht Design / D-Ulm / 168 Punkte/*Points*	10

Siemens-Electrogeräte GmbH
Designabteilung (MDS)

Anschrift/*Address*
Postfach 10 02 50
D-80076 München
Ansprechpartner/*Contact*
Gerd E. Wilsdorf
Telefon/*Phone*
+49 (0)89/45 90-32 35
Telefax/*Fax*
+49 (0)89/45 90-298
Mitarbeiter/*Employees*
12

Bei der Entwicklung neuer Produkte und Lösungen gilt für Siemens seit Generationen das selbe Credo: es den Menschen ihn ihrem Zuhause bequemer, leichter und sicherer zu machen und ihnen gleichzeitig die Möglichkeit zu geben, ihre Individualität zu leben und zu genießen. Dieses Credo gilt auch für die Designabteilung der Siemens-Electrogeräte GmbH. Mit einer zeitlos modernen Formensprache, klaren Strukturen, geordneten geometrischen Grundformen sowie den entsprechenden Materialien erreichen wir eine höchstmögliche Funktionalität unserer Geräte. Die Form folgt der Funktion, das Design ermöglicht eine einfache Bedienung.

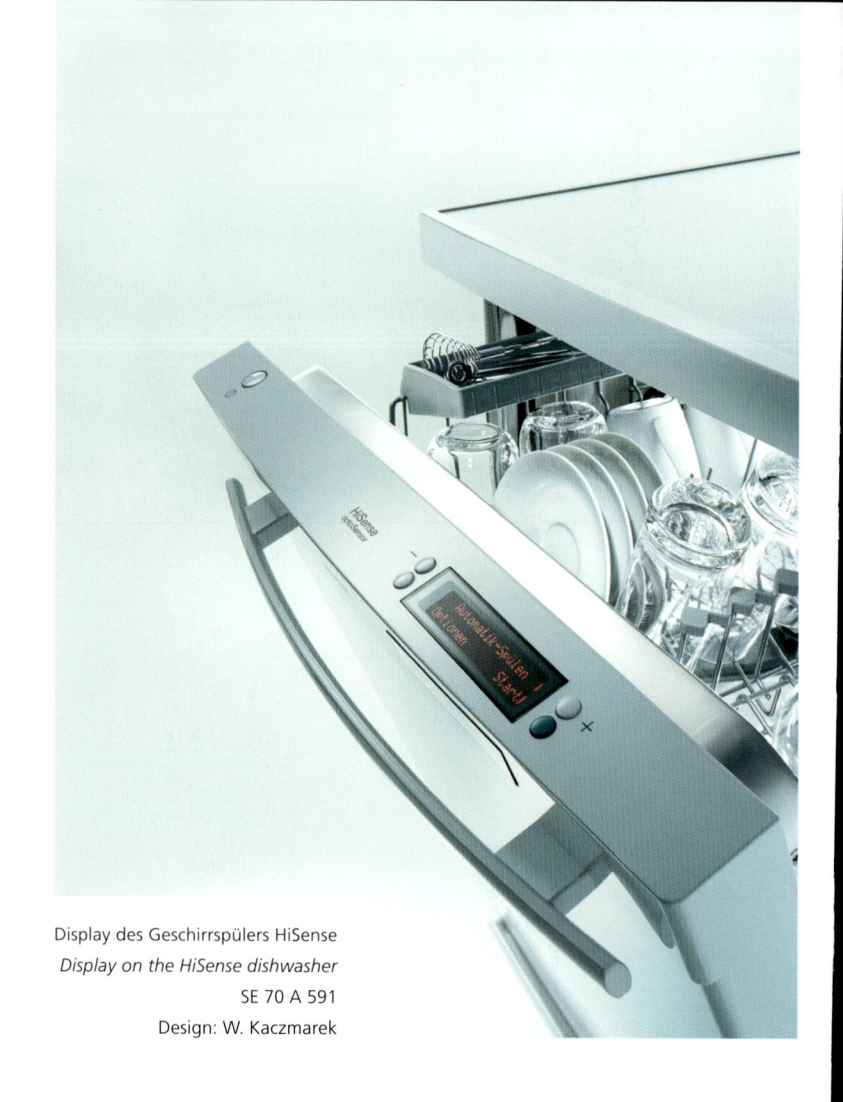

Display des Geschirrspülers HiSense
Display on the HiSense dishwasher
SE 70 A 591
Design: W. Kaczmarek

Waschmaschine serie IQ mit Klartext-Display
serie IQ washing machine with plain-text display
WIQ 1630
Design: J. Geyer, Gerd E. Wilsdorf

In the development of new products and solutions Siemens has applied the same principle for generations: to make things more comfortable, easier and safer for people at home and at the same time to give them the opportunity to experience and enjoy their individuality.
This principle also applies to the Design Department of Siemens Electrogeräte GmbH.
With a timelessly modern design approach, clear structures, a system of basic geometric shapes and the corresponding materials we achieve the highest possible level of functionality for our appliances. The form follows the function, the design ensures easy operation.

Glaskeramik-Kochfeld mit koch- und bratSensor
Glas-ceramic hob with boiling and frying sensor
EK 78 H 55, EK 73 H 55
Design: Gerd E. Wilsdorf

Einbau-Kompakt-Backofen quantumSpeed sowie Dampfgarer
quantumSpeed built-in compact oven and steamer
HB 77 L 55, HB 28 D 55
Design: F. Rieser, Gerd E. Wilsdorf

Siemens-Electrogeräte

Haushalt, Küche und Bad/ Household, Kitchen and Bath

Siemens-Electrogeräte GmbH
Designabteilung (MDS)

Anschrift/*Address*
Postfach 10 02 50
D-80076 München
Ansprechpartner/*Contact*
Gerd E. Wilsdorf
Telefon/*Phone*
+49 (0)89/45 90-32 35
Telefax/*Fax*
+49 (0)89/45 90-298
Mitarbeiter/*Employees*
12

Der souveräne Einsatz edler Materialien wie Aluminium, Edelstahl und Glas verbindet sich bei Siemens Geräten zu einem außergewöhnlichen Ganzen. Wie bei der **s-line**® von Siemens. Ein bis ins kleinste Detail unvergleichliches Geräteprogramm. Die flachen Gerätefronten kombiniert mit Schwarzglas und gebogenem Profilgriff zeichnen einen klaren, puristischen Designstil.

Auch der neue Einbau-Wein-Kühlschrank VinoThek sowie der Gas-Einbauherd setzen optische Highlights in Edelstahl und Glas.

Einbauherd mit Backwagen der **s-line**®
s-line® built-in cooker with baking trolley
HE 68 E 75
Design: Gerd E. Wilsdorf

Einbau-Wein-Kühlschrank VinoThek
in Edelstahloptik
VinoThek built-in wine refrigerator
in stainless-steel look
KF 18 W 420
Design: C. Becke

Aluminium-Esse der **s-line**®
s-line® aluminium hood
LC 86972
Design: Gerd E. Wilsdorf

Elektro-Einbauherd mit Gaskochfeld
Built-in electric cooker with gas burner
HK 48054, EG 71464
Design: F. Rieser, Gerd E. Wilsdorf

*The masterly use of high-quality materials such as aluminium, stainless steel and glass in the manufacture of Siemens appliances produces exceptional units. As in the **s-line**® from Siemens. An appliance range witch down to the smallest detail is incomparable. The flat appliance fronts combined with black glass and arched profile handle form a clear, puristic design style.*

The new VinoThek built-in wine refrigerator and the built-in gas cooker also create optical highlights in stainless steel and glass.

Haushalt, Küche und Bad / Household, Kitchen and Bath

Siemens-Electrogeräte

Sympathische Grundwerte in Verbindung mit überragender Technik – so versteht sich die moderne Marke BOSCH in ihrer Tradition.

Die hohe, verlässliche Qualität der Geräte besteht auf ständig verbesserten Materialien und Oberflächen, herausragenden Ingenieurleistungen und langjährige vielfältige Erfahrungen.

Die sich selbsterklärenden, logisch und verständlich gestalteten Bedieneinheiten bieten höchsten Kundennutzen und bewirken zugleich eine Faszination und Akzeptanz modernster Technik.

Schonung der natürlichen Ressourcen, nicht nur im Herstellungsprozess der Geräte, sondern speziell im alltäglichen Gebrauch sind oberstes Gebot der Marke BOSCH.

Die zeitgemäße, moderne Formensprache, perfekt modulierte Greifformen, kontrastreiche Anzeigeelemente, präzise stabile Formverbindungen und größtmögliche Servicefreundlichkeit prägen den unverwechselbaren Charakter der BOSCH-Hausgeräte.

Robert Bosch Hausgeräte GmbH

Anschrift/*Address*
Hochstraße 17
D-81669 München

Ansprechpartner/*Contact*
Presse: Uta Rodenhäuser

Telefon/*Phone*
+49 (0)89/45 90-28 08

Ansprechpartner/*Contact*
Design: Roland Vetter

Telefon/*Phone*
+49 (0)7322/92-25 52

Telefax/*Fax*
+49 (0)89/45 90-29 57

E-mail/*E-mail*
bosch-pr@bshg.com

Internet/*Website*
www.bosch-hausgeraete.de

HBN 9650 Einbau-Doppelbackofen/
Built-in double oven

PCL 785 F Gas-Kochstelle/*Gas hob*

HSW 195 A EU Solitaire-Standherd/
Solitaire Cooker

Appealing fundamental values in conjunction with outstanding technology - this is how the modern brand, BOSCH regards itself in terms of its tradition.

The high, reliable quality of the appliances is based on continuously improved materials and surface finishes, outstanding engineering and many years of varied experience.

The self-explanatory, logical and comprehensively designed operating controls offer maximum user-friendliness and simultaneously, inspire a fascination for and acceptance of advanced technology.

Husbanding natural resources, not only in the product manufacturing process but in daily use, especially, is the central precept of the BOSCH brand.

The contemporary modern design language, perfectly fashioned handle styles, richly contrasted display elements, precise, stable style combinations and the greatest possible service-friendliness mark the distinctive character of BOSCH domestic appliances.

Haushalt, Küche und Bad/Household, Kitchen and Bath

Robert Bosch Hausgeräte

Haushalt, Küche und Bad/*Household, Kitchen and Bathroom*

Miele

Miele & Cie.

Anschrift/*Address*
Carl-Miele-Straße 29
D-33332 Gütersloh

Ansprechpartner/*Contact*
Frido Jacobs

Telefon/*Phone*
+49 (0)5241/89-41 41

Telefax/*Fax*
+49 (0)5241/89-41 40

E-mail/*E-mail*
info@miele.de

Internet/*Website*
www.miele.de

Gründungsdatum/*Foundation*
1899

Umsatz/*Turnover*
2,24 Milliarden Euro
(Geschäftsjahr 2001/2002)

Mitarbeiterzahl/*Employees*
15.328

Kunden/*Clients*
Fachhandel
Specialist dealers

Filialen/*Branch Offices*
14 Vertriebszentren
in Deutschland
31 ausländische
Vertriebsniederlassungen
14 Area Sales Offices in Germany
31 Foreign Subsidiaries

"Klasse statt Masse", oder anders ausgedrückt Qualität statt Quantität, bestimmt die Erfolgsformel des Unternehmens Miele & Cie. seit der Gründung 1899. Mit diesem Unternehmensgrundsatz hat sich das Familienunternehmen Miele den Weg zu einem der führenden europäischen Hausgerätehersteller bereitet - durch Konzentration auf ein Geräteangebot mit hohem Leistungsniveau und richtungsweisender Technologie. Durch das Streben hin zu Qualitätsprodukten mit fortschrittlicher Hausgerätetechnik und einem immer höheren Gebrauchsnutzen ist Miele zu einem Markenanbieter geworden, der sich aus der Masse des Marktangebotes hervorhebt: Modernste Technik, fortschrittliches Design und die sprichwörtliche Langlebigkeit der Produkte werden unterstrichen durch ein Höchstmaß an Funktionalität und Gebrauchsnutzen. Das Produktspektrum umfasst u.a. Waschmaschinen, Wäschetrockner, Geschirrspüler, Küchen-Einbau- und -Standgeräte zum Kochen und Kühlen, Staubsauger sowie gewerbliche Wäschepflege- und Spülgeräte.

Dunstabzugshaube DA 279
Cooker hood DA 279

Dunstabzugshaube DA 289
„Kopffreiheit"
Cooker hood DA 289
„Headroom"

Kochmulde KM 550
Hob unit KM 550

Kochmulde KM 548
Hob unit KM 548

The maxim "Quality rather than quantity" has been the formula for success at Miele & Cie. ever since the company was founded in 1899. This philosophy has paved the way for the family-run company Miele to become one of the leading white goods manufacturers in Europe, success achieved thanks to concentration on an appliance range offering the highest quality standards and future-proof technology. By endeavoring to produce quality products equipped with state-of-the-art household appliance technology and an increasing number of user benefits, Miele has become a supplier who stands head and shoulders above the mass of other brands on the market: state-of-the-art technology, progressive design and products renowned for their durability go hand in glove with a high degree of functionality and user convenience. The product range includes washing machines, tumble dryers, dishwashers, built-in and freestanding kitchen appliances for cooking and refrigeration, vacuum cleaners as well as commercial laundry-care machines and dishwashers.

Staubsauger „Seventy-five"
Vacuum cleaner „Seventy-five"

Tools Design

Anschrift/*Address*
Rentemestervej 23A
DK-2400 Copenhagen NV
Denmark

Ansprechpartner/*Contact*
Claus Jensen und Henrik Holbaek

Telefon/*Phone*
+45 38 19 41 14

Telefax/*Fax*
+45 38 19 41 13

E-mail/*E-mail*
email@toolsdesign.dk

Internet/*Website*
www.toolsdesign.com

Gründungsdatum/*Foundation*
1989

Mitarbeiter/*Employees*
2

Kunden/*Clients*
Eva Solo/Eva Denmark A/S,
George Jensen/
Royal Scandinavia A/S,
Tommy Larsen A/S, Ambu A/S,
BarcoNet A/S a.o.

Ausstattung/*Equipment*
3-D, DTP, Animation/Film,
Modellbau, Video/Fotostudio
3-D, DTP, Animation/Movie, Model workshop, Video/Photo studio

Tätigkeitsfelder/*Fields of Activity*
Industrie-Design, Produkt-Design,
Life Style Design, Corporate Design,
Grafik-Design, Verpackung
Industrial design, Product design, Life style design, Corporate design, Graphic design, Packaging

Tools Design gehört mit mehr als 45 Preisen und Auszeichnungen zu den besten Designern Dänemarks und vertritt dänisches Design auf verschiedenen internationalen Ausstellungen.
Die Produkte von Tools Design sind häufig gekennzeichnet durch eine einfache und innovative Betrachtungsweise. Die Produktpalette reicht von elektronischen über medizinische Geräte bis hin zu Haushaltsgeräten.
Die Design Philosophie von Tools Design ist es, den Produkten das „gewisse Extra" zu verleihen. Die Stärke des Studios besteht darin, Produkt-Design und Kommunikation zu verbinden, um Lifestyle-Design zu erschaffen.

With more than 45 awards and distinctions Tools Design rank amongst Denmarks most awarded designers. They have represented Danish design on several international exhibitions.

The products of Tools Design are often characterized by a simplistic and innovative approach.
The portfolio ranges from electronics and medical equipment to household products.

The design philosophy of Tools Design is to put „something extra" into the products. The strength of the studio is to manage product design and communication to create lifestyle design.

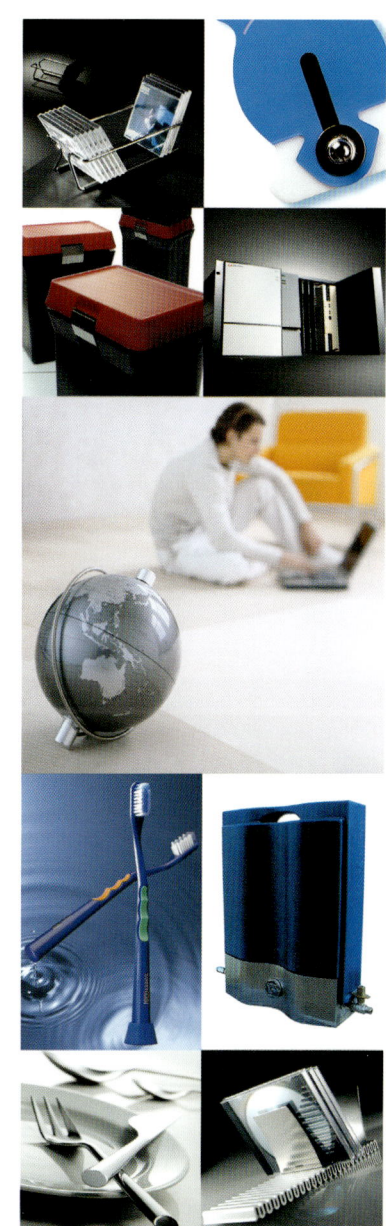

Haushalt, Küche und Bad/Household, Kitchen and Bath

Tools Design 6

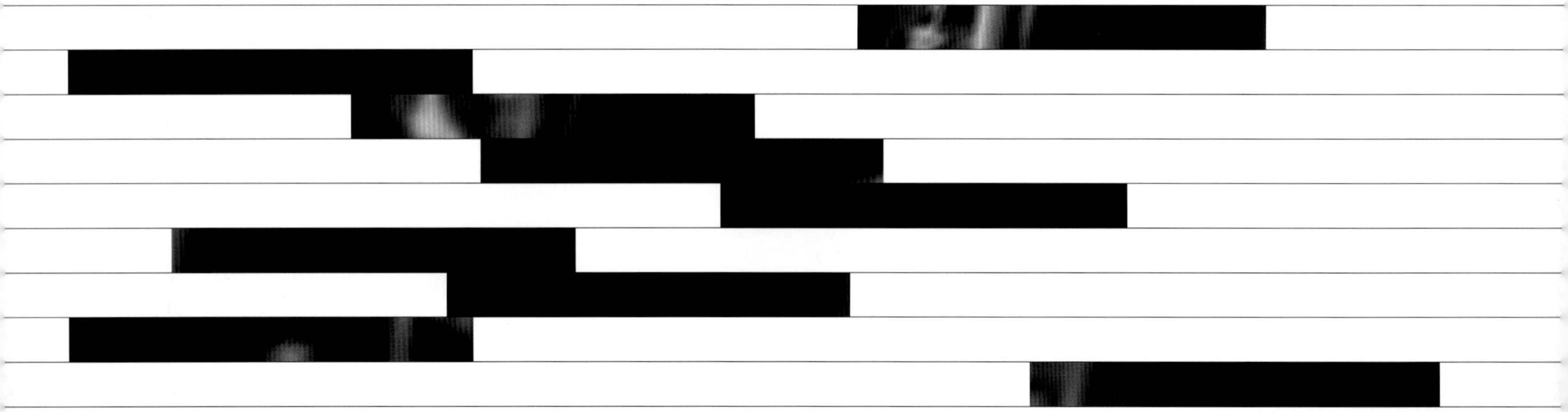

Public Design
Public Design

Rang/*Rank*

Roy Fleetwood / GB-Cambridge / 192 Punkte/*Points*	1
Prof. Josef P. Kleihues / D-Berlin / 192 Punkte/*Points*	1
Wall / D-Berlin / 192 Punkte/*Points*	1
Jasper Morrison Office for Design / GB-London / 162 Punkte/*Points*	4
wiege Entwicklungsges. / D-Bad Münder / 154 Punkte/*Points*	5
Hawle Armaturen / D-Freilassing / 144 Punkte/*Points*	6
nlplk industrial design / NL-Leiden / 128 Punkte/*Points*	7
SPECTRAL GESELLSCHAFT FÜR LICHTTECHNIK / D-Freiburg / 128 Punkte/*Points*	7
Studio Arch. Michele de Lucchi / I-Mailand / 124 Punkte/*Points*	9
Leitner / D-Waiblingen / 106 Punkte/*Points*	10

# Freizeit, Sport und Spiel
Leisure, Sport and Play

Rang/*Rank*

Cognito Design und Engineering / D-Oberhausen-Rheinhausen / 292 Punkte/*Points*	1
BMW / D-München / 286 Punkte/*Points*	2
Volkswagen / D-Wolfsburg / 256 Punkte/*Points*	3
yellow circle / D-Köln / 256 Punkte/*Points*	3
Teams Design / D-Esslingen / 192 Punkte/*Points*	5
SRAM / D-Schweinfurt / 148 Punkte/*Points*	6
Fiskars Consumer / FIN-Billnäs / 144 Punkte/*Points*	7
SNIKE Sport / D-Stuttgart / 140 Punkte/*Points*	8
Vistapark / D-Wuppertal / 106 Punkte/*Points*	9
Micro Mobility Systems / CH-Küsnacht / 84 Punkte/*Points*	10

Freizeit, Sport und Spiel/*Leisure, Sports and Play*

BMW AG

Anschrift/*Address*
D-80788 München
Ansprechpartner/*Contact*
Abteilung Öffentlichkeitsarbeit
Public Relation Department
Telefon/*Phone*
+49 (0)89/38 20
Internet/*Website*
www.BMWgroup.de

Der BMW StreetCarver, ein Fun-Sportgerät für die Skater Generation, das auch Scarven auf der Asphaltpiste möglich macht.

Fahrwerks-Komponenten aus dem 5er BMW, innovative Materialien und eine ausgeklügelte Lenkungstechnik machen den Streetcarver zusammen mit seinem klaren und doch emotionalen Design zu einem neuen Trend-Sport-Gerät.

The BMW StreetCarver belongs to the Skater generation and even enables scarving on the asphalt runway.

With its chassis components from the BMW 5 Series, innovative materials and an ingenious steering system technology the BMW StreetCarver is a new trend sport vehicle. Its clear but emotional design reflects the BMW Design Philosophy.

Freizeit, Sport und Spiel/*Leisure, Sports and Play*

Micro Mobility

Das 3. Jahrtausend und das Zeitalter der Micro Mobilität ist eingeläutet. Der neue Lifestyle heißt Fortbewegung, Sport, Natur und vor allem Spaß ...

Micro Mobility Systems hat die Vision, in Zukunft diesen Lifestyle mitzuprägen. Als Erfinder des Kickboards® und des Original micro® Scooters haben wir in Sachen Innovation und High-End Produkten unbestritten die Nase vorn. Technologisch und qualitativ hochstehende Produkte mit Schweizer Design sind unser Erfolgsrezept. Kickboard® und micro® sind unsere eingetragenen Marken.

Micro Mobility Systems AG

Anschrift/*Address*
Bahnhofstraße 10
CH-8700 Küsnacht/Zürich

Ansprechpartner/*Contact*
Wim Ouboter

Telefon/*Phone*
+41 (0)1/91 01 122

Telefax/*Fax*
+41 (0)1/91 06 629

E-mail/*E-mail*
w.ouboter@micro-mobility.com

Internet/*Website*
www.micro-mobility.com

Gründungsdatum/*Foundation*
1996

Mitarbeiter/*Employees*
6

Kunden/*Clients*
Sportfachhandel, K2, IKEA,
Schweizer Militär
Sports retail, K2, IKEA, Swiss army

Tätigkeitsfelder/*Fields of Activity*
Entwicklung und Vermarktung von Trendprodukten für Sport, Lifestyle und Micro Mobilität
Development and marketing of trendy equipment for sports, lifestyle and micro mobility

Warnung:
Dies ist kein Spielzeug,
sondern ein trendiges Sportgerät.
Warning:
This is not a toy
but a trendy sport equipment.

Mini micro® Kickboard®:
An Sicherheits- und ergonomische Bedürfnisse von Kindern ab 3 Jahren angepasst. Sinnvoll für Gleichgewichts- und Bewegungstraining.

Mini micro® Kickboard®:
Sensibly adapted to the safety and ergonomic requirements of children from the age of 3 years. Good for training balance and movement.

micro® Skate Scooter:

Ist weltweit zu einem Trend in Sport und Lifestyle geworden. Kein Produkt hat zuvor von der Schweiz aus in so kurzer Zeit die Welt erobert.

micro® Skate Scooter:

Has become a worldwide trend in sports and lifestyle. No other product has captured the world in such a short period of time out of Switzerland.

We have now entered the 3rd millennium and the age of micro mobility. The new lifestyle is dedicated to movement and means, sports, nature and above all enjoyment ...

Micro Mobility Systems has the vision of playing a major role in this lifestyle in future. As inventor of the kickboard and the original micro® Scooter we are undoubtedly leaders in innovation and hi-end products. High quality and technologically superior products with Swiss design are our recipe for success. Kichboard® and micro® are our famous trade marks.

micro® Kickboard®:

Aluminium-Konstruktion mit konvexem GFK-Holz-Flexdeck, modularer Aufbau. So können individuell und nach eigenen Ansprüchen mit wenigen Handgriffen Decks, Rollen und komplette Hinterteile gewechselt werden.

micro® Kickboard®:

Aluminium construction with a convex fibreglass-wood sandwich deck. Modular structure. This allows decks, wheels and complete rear sections to be exchanged according to individual requirements with a minimum of effort.

micro® Flex Scooter®:

Aluminium-Konstruktion mit konvexem GFK-Holz-Flexdeck, modularer Aufbau. So können individuell und nach eigenen Ansprüchen mit wenigen Handgriffen Decks, Rollen und komplette Hinterteile gewechselt werden.

micro® Flex®:

Aluminium construction with a convex fibreglass-wood sandwich deck. Modular structure. This allows decks, wheels and complete rear sections to be exchanged according to individual requirements with a minimum of effort.

Accessoires
Accessories

Rang/*Rank*

Atelier Eva Katharina Bruggmann / CH-Zürich / 208 Punkte/*Points*	1
Ferdinand Menrad / D-Krailing / 208 Punkte/*Points*	1
Silhouette International Schmied / A-Linz / 208 Punkte/*Points*	1
Philippe Starck / F-Issy les Moulineaux / 160 Punkte/*Points*	4
Rolf Hertkorn Design / D-Ravensburg / 128 Punkte/*Points*	5
Samsonite Europe / B-Oudenaarde / 128 Punkte/*Points*	5
Wilkinson Sword / D-Solingen / 128 Punkte/*Points*	5
deSIGN Markus T. / D-Gütersloh / 124 Punkte/*Points*	8
BREE Collection / D-Isernhagen / 106 Punkte/*Points*	9
Ergonomi Design / S-Bromma / 106 Punkte/*Points*	9

Gesamt-Ranking: Top 20
Overall Ranking: Top 20

Rang/*Rank*

Phoenix Product Design / D-Stuttgart / 1732 Punkte/*Points*	1
IBM / D-Herrenberg / 1424 Punkte/*Points*	2
Sony / D-Berlin / 1376 Punkte/*Points*	3
Teams Design / D-Esslingen / 1232 Punkte/*Points*	4
Festo / D-Denkendorf / 1067 Punkte/*Points*	5
designafairs / D-München / 1010 Punkte/*Points*	6
Siemens-Electrogeräte / D-München / 938 Punkte/*Points*	7
BMW / D-München / 898 Punkte/*Points*	8
Samsung Electronics / D-Schwalbach / 712 Punkte/*Points*	9
MA Design / D-Kiel / 606 Punkte/*Points*	10
Ergonomi Design / S-Bromma / 530 Punkte/*Points*	11
Neumeister Design / D-München / 520 Punkte/*Points*	12
Canon / D-Krefeld / 512 Punkte/*Points*	13
Volkswagen / D-Wolfsburg / 484 Punkte/*Points*	14
wiege Entwicklungsges. / D-Bad Münder / 474 Punkte/*Points*	15
Studio Ambrozus / D-Köln / 464 Punkte/*Points*	16
SPECTRAL GESELLSCHAFT FÜR LICHTTECHNIK / D-Freiburg / 464 Punkte/*Points*	16
Heidelberger Druckmaschinen / D-Heidelberg / 456 Punkte/*Points*	18
Design Tech Jürgen R. Schmid / D-Ammerbuch / 440 Punkte/*Points*	19
Apple Computer / D-Feldkirchen / 400 Punkte/*Points*	20

Phoenix Product Design
Stuttgart/Tokyo

Anschrift/*Address*
Kölner Straße 16
D-70376 Stuttgart

Ansprechpartner/*Contact*
Andreas Haug
Tom Schönherr
Andreas Dimitriadis

Telefon/*Phone*
+49 (0)711/95 59 760

Telefax/*Fax*
+49 (0)711/55 93 92

E-mail/*E-mail*
info@phoenixdesign.de

Internet/*Website*
phoenixdesign.de

Gründungsdatum/*Foundation*
1987

Filiale/*Branch Office*
Hiroshi Otsuka
3-23-7-706 Motonakayama
J-Funabashi-shi, Chiba 273

Telefon/*Phone*
+81 (0)473/36 68 97

Telefax/*Fax*
+81 (0)473/36 58 57

E-mail/*E-mail*
Hiroshi.Otsuka@phoenixdesign.de

Mitarbeiter/*Employees*
17

Kunden/*Clients*
AEG, Alape, Axor, Duravit, Fuji, Xerox, Gaggenau, Grundig, Gira, Hagenuk, Hansgrohe, Häfele, IBM, Kaldewei, Lamy, Leonardo, Loewe, Mexx, Miele, Pharo, Shock, Sharp, Tchibo, Viessmann

Ausstattung/*Equipment*
Inhouse CAID (Alias Wavefront, SolidWorks, Rhinoceros),
NC Bearbeitung, Modellbau, Fotostudio
Inhouse CAID (Alias Wavefront, SolidWorks, Rhinoceros), NC processing, model making, photo studio

Tätigkeitsfelder/*Fields of Activity*
Strategische Design-Beratung, Productdesign, Zukunftskonzepte, Experimentelles Design
Strategic design consulting, product design, future concepts, experimental design

In den besten Traditionen klassischen deutschen Designs liegen die Wurzeln des Erfolgs von Phoenix Product Design. Tom Schönherr und Andreas Haug, Gründer und Inhaber des Unternehmens folgen deshalb weder Doktrinen noch kurzlebigen Trends oder Moden, sondern definieren ihre Design-Philosophie als eine Haltung. Zu den Grundwerten dieser Haltung zählen Ethik und Ästhetik, Ökonomie, Präzision und Konkretheit sowie die Interessen von Hersteller, Marke und Verbraucher. Ziel der Designer sind nicht die solitären Sensationen, sondern die strategische Design-Beratung, die Unternehmen, ihre Marken und ihre Produkte unverwechselbar und wettbewerbsfähig im Markt positioniert. Das Ergebnis sind Produkte, die sich auszeichnen durch Logik, Moral und Magie. Die Logik schließt Qualitäten ein, wie moderne Werkstoffe und Fertigungstechnologien, angemessener Preis und Benutzerfreundlichkeit. Die Moral übernimmt Verantwortung für die Umwelt, das Unternehmen, seine Mitarbeiter, seine Marktpartner und die Endverbraucher. Die Magie schließlich ist jene Kraft aus Form und Idee, die die Mitarbeiter motiviert und die Käufer verzaubert.

Loewe Certos

Mexx Passion

Xerox Phaser

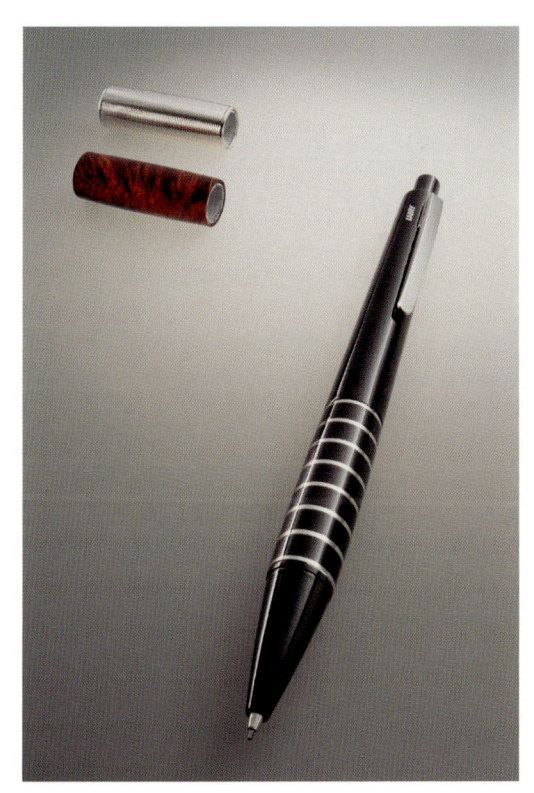

Lamy Accent

Hansgrohe Raindance

The success of Phoenix Product Design has its roots in the best traditions of classic German design. Tom Schönherr and Andreas Haug, founders and owners of the enterprise pursue neither doctrines nor short-lived trends or fashions, but rather define their design philosophy as an attitude. The basic values of this attitude include ethics and aesthetics, economy and ecology, precision and concreteness as well as the interests of manufacturer, market and consumer. Their designer's goal is not the solitary sensation, but rather to position unmistakably and competitively the strategic design consultation, the company, its brands and its products. The resulting products are distinguished by logic, morality and magic. The logic includes qualities such as modern materials, and production technologies, reasonable prices and user friendliness. Morality implies responsibility for the environment, the enterprise, its employees, its market partners and the end customer. Finally, magic is that power from form and idea which motivates the employees and charms the purchaser.

Teams Design

Anschrift/*Address*
Kollwitzstraße 1
D-73728 Esslingen

Geschäftsführung/*Management*
Reinhard Renner
Hans Peter Aglassinger
Klaus Baumgartner

Telefon/*Phone*
+49 (0)711/35 17 65-0

Telefax/*Fax*
+49 (0)711/35 17 65-25

E-mail/*E-mail*
info@teams-design.de

Internet/*Website*
www.teamsdesign.de

Gründungsdatum/*Foundation*
1956 als Slany Design durch
Prof. H.E. Slany
1987 Verbreiterung der
Aktionsbasis durch Aufnahme
von R. Renner und K. Schön in
die Geschäftsführung
1998 Gründung von Teams Design,
USA, mit Sitz in Chicago
2002 Gründung von Teams Design,
Hamburg
1956 as Slany Design by
Prof. H.E. Slany
1987 Expansion of the leadership
by appointing R. Renner and
K. Schön to the board
1998 Founding of Teams Design,
USA in Chicago
2002 Founding of Teams Design,
Hamburg

Mitarbeiter/*Employees*
34

Ausstattung/*Equipment*
CAD, Modellbau, DTP
CAD, model making, DTP

Firmenphilosophie
Seit über 40 Jahren werden wir mit der Gestaltung von industriell gefertigten Produkten beauftragt und gehören zu den erfahrensten und profiliertesten Design-Teams. Mit 34 Mitarbeitern zählen wir zu den größten Designagenturen. Das Team ist international besetzt. Unser Team hat bisher annähernd 1000 nationale und internationale Designauszeichnungen für realisierte Produkte erhalten – verliehen von internationalen Jurys. Das ist weltweit einmalig.
Viele von uns gestaltete Produkte erhielten Auszeichnungen für Langzeit-Design.
1990 Design Team des Jahres (Design Zentrum Nordrhein Westfalen)
1996 Platz 2 der Gesamtwertung im Ranking Top Ten International (Design Zentrum Nordrhein Westfalen)
1997 Ranking:Design (d…c Unternehmensberatung) Platz 2 im Gesamtranking. Platz 1 in der Kategorie Handwerk und Industrie.
In 3 weiteren Kategorien jeweils unter den ersten 10.
1998/99 Platz 1 in der Kategorie Handwerk und Industrie (Ranking:Design)
1999 Designpreis des Jahrzehnts von Business Week und IDSA

Referenzen
Einmalig ist, dass die Mehrzahl unserer Kunden seit vielen Jahrzehnten mit uns zusammenarbeitet. Auf den Gebieten Investitionsgüter und Konsumgüter sind wir für Konzerne und mittelständische Unternehmen tätig, die auf ihren Gebieten in der Regel Marktführer sind.
Zum Beispiel: Bosch (seit 1957), Leifheit (seit 1959), Silit (seit 1962), Kärcher (seit 1964), Leitz (seit 1973), Still (seit 1987), Weishaupt (seit 1987), Wolfcraft (seit 1997).

TEAMS DESIGN | ESSLINGEN | HAMBURG | CHICAGO

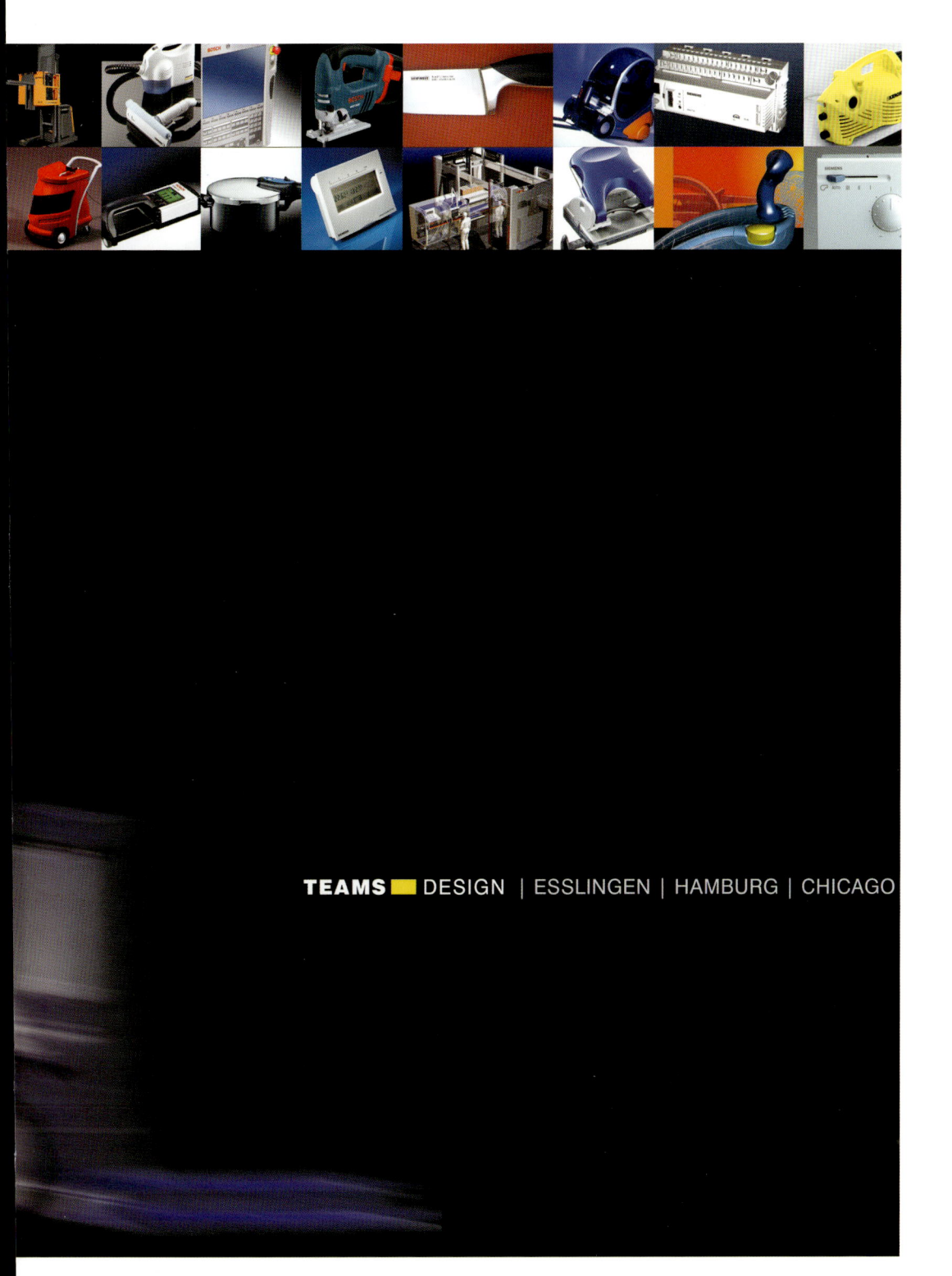

Corporate Philosophy
For over 40 years we have been receiving commissions for the design of industrially produced goods and are among the most experienced and distinguished design agencies. The Team consists of an international staff.
Our Team has thus far received almost 1000 national and international design awards for realized products – awarded by international juries. Many products designed by us have received awards for longterm design.
1990 Design Team of the Year (Design Center Northrhine Westphalia)
1996 2nd place in the Ranking Top Ten International (Design Center Northrhine Westphalia)
1997 Ranking:Design (d...c brand + design consultants) rank 2 in the overall ranking. Rank 1 in the trade and industry category, among the top ten in 3 other categories.
1998 1st place in the trade and industry category (Ranking:Design)
1999 Design of the decades award (Business Week and IDSA).

References
What's unique is that most of our clients have been working with us for decades. We are working for large cooperations and medium-sized enterprises who generally are market leaders in their industries in the fields of investment goods and consumer goods. For example: Bosch (since 1957), Leifheit (since 1959), Silit (since 1962), Kärcher (since 1964), Leitz (since 1973), Still (since 1987), Weishaupt (since 1987),Wolfcraft (since 1997).

Festo AG & Co. KG
Corporate Design

Anschrift/*Address*
Rechbergstraße 3
D-73770 Denkendorf
Ansprechpartner/*Contact*
Prof. Dipl.-Ing. Axel Thallemer
Head of Corporate Design
Telefon/*Phone*
+49(0)711/3 47 38 80
Telefax/*Fax*
+49(0)711/3 47 38 99
E-mail/*E-mail*
tem@festo.com

Design Team of the Year 2001

Festo

Hall of Fame
Industrie-Design/*Industrial Design*

Legend: 1996/97 (orange), 1997/98 (teal), 1998/99 (yellow), 1999/00 (lavender), 2001/02 (olive), 2002/03 (red)

Platzierungen/*Placements* 1996–2003 | Gesamtpunkte/*Total points* | Rang/*Rank*

Handwerk und Industrie/*Trade and Industry*

Firma	1996/97	1997/98	1998/99	1999/00	2001/02	2002/03	Gesamtpunkte	Rang
Festo / D-Denkendorf	●	●	●	●	●	●	4005	1
Teams Design / D-Esslingen	●	●	●	●	●	●	2845	2
Phoenix Product Design / D-Stuttgart				●	●		1474	3
designpraxis diener / D-Ulm	●		●		●	●	1214	4
Studiowerk Design / D-Inning	●				●	●	800	5
designafairs / D-München	●	●		●			644	6
Viessmann Werke / D-Allendorf				●			584	7
Scala Design / D-Böblingen		●	●				504	8
busse design / D-Elchingen	●	●					478	9
Heidelberger Druckmaschinen / D-Heidelberg						●	456	10

Medizin und Rehabilitation/*Medicine and Rehabilitation*

Firma	1996/97	1997/98	1998/99	1999/00	2001/02	2002/03	Gesamtpunkte	Rang
designafairs / D-München	●	●	●	●	●	●	1886	1
Held + Team / D-Hamburg				●	●	●	1050	2
Philips Design / NL-Eindhoven	●	●			●		708	3
piu products / D-Essen					●	●	544	4
Windi Winderlich Design / D-Hamburg	●	●					460	5
einmaleins - Büro für Gestaltung / D-Burgrieden					●	●	440	6
Koop Industrial Design / D-Hamburg			●	●	●		402	7
Pilotprojekt / D-Münster				●	●	●	400	8
Design Tech Jürgen R. Schmid / D-Ammerbuch	●		●				314	9
OCO-Design / D-Münster	●	●		●			308	10

Medien, Kommunikation und Unterhaltungselektronik/
Media, Communication and Entertainment Electronics

Sony Europe / D-Berlin	●	●	●	●	●	●	4944	1
IBM / D-Herrenberg	●	●	●		●	●	3880	2
designafairas / D-München	●	●	●	●	●	●	2284	3
Phoenix Product Design / D-Stuttgart	●	●	●	●	●	●	2124	4
Philips Design / NL-Eindhoven		●	●	●	●	●	1672	5
Ideo Product Development / GB-London	●	●	●				1096	6
MA Design / D-Kiel	●			●	●	●	1078	7
Samsung Electronics / D-Schwalbach					●	●	1008	8
Ziba Design / USA-Portland	●	●	●	●			1000	9
Canon / D-Krefeld		●		●		●	960	10

Verkehrsmittel und Sonderfahrzeuge/
Transportation and Special Use Vehicles

BMW / D-München	●	●	●	●	●	●	1934	1
DaimlerChrysler / D-Sindelfingen	●	●	●	●	●	●	1506	2
Audi / D-Ingolstadt	●	●	●	●	●	●	1350	3
Volkswagen / D-Wolfsburg	●	●	●	●	●		976	4
Dr. Ing. h.c. F. Porsche / D-Stuttgart	●	●		●	●	●	972	5
Neumeister Design / D-München	●				●	●	624	6
Recaro / D-Kirchheim-Teck		●	●	●			402	7
Crown Gabelstapler / D-München	●					●	384	8
Designworks/USA / D-München					●	●	344	9
Deutsche Bahn / D-Berlin						●	228	10

Büro und Objekt/
Office and Public Space

SPECTRAL GES. FÜR LICHTTECHNIK / D-Freiburg			●	●	●	●	1426	1
wiege Entwicklungsges. / D-Bad Münder	●	●	●			●	948	2
Jorge Pensi / E-Barcelona		●	●	●			662	3
Foster and Partners / GB-London					●	●	634	4
Vorwerk / D-Wuppertal		●			●		448	5
designafairs / D-München					●	●	440	6
Sedus Stoll / D-Waldshut				●		●	392	7
Tobias Grau / D-Hamburg		●	●				364	8
BEGA Gantenbrink-Leuchten / D-Menden	●		●				352	9
Fabian Industrie Design / D-Mannheim	●	●					342	10

Hall of Fame
Industrie-Design/*Industrial Design*

Legend: 🟠 1996/97 · 🔵 1997/98 · 🟡 1998/99 · 🟣 1999/00 · 🟨 2001/02 · 🔴 2002/03

Wohnung/
Living

Name	1996/97	1997/98	1998/99	1999/00	2001/02	2002/03	Gesamtpunkte/*Total points* 1996–2003	Rang/*Rank*
nya nordiska / D-Dannenberg	🟠	🔵	🟡	🟣	🟨	🔴	1552	1
Peter Maly / D-Hamburg			🟡		🟨	🔴	460	2
Phoenix Product Design / D-Stuttgart						🔴	444	3
FSB Franz Schneider Brakel / D-Brakel				🟣	🟨		294	4
Jakob Gebert / D-Weil am Rhein		🔵	🟡				276	5
Tobias Grau / D-Hamburg	🟠			🟣			248	6
Kurt Ernie / CH-Willisau					🟨		224	7
Wellis / CH-Willisau					🟨		224	7
designafairs / D-München					🟨		192	9
Gira Giersiepen / D-Radevormwald				🟣			184	10
Zecca + Zecca / I-Milano	🟠						184	10

Haushalt, Küche und Bad/
Household, Kitchen and Bathroom

Name	1996/97	1997/98	1998/99	1999/00	2001/02	2002/03	Gesamtpunkte/*Total points* 1996–2003	Rang/*Rank*
Siemens Electrogeräte / D-München			🟡	🟣	🟨	🔴	3420	1
Phoenix Product Design / D-Stuttgart	🟠	🔵	🟡	🟣		🔴	2072	2
Philips Design / NL-Eindhoven	🟠	🔵	🟡	🟣	🟨		1544	3
Miele & Cie. / D-Gütersloh	🟠	🔵	🟡		🟨	🔴	1480	4
Studio Ambrozus / D-Köln				🟣	🟨	🔴	1418	5
Robert Bosch Hausgeräte / D-München			🟡		🟨	🔴	1300	6
Braun / D-Kronberg	🟠	🔵	🟡				1179	7
Teams Design / D-Esslingen	🟠					🔴	664	8
Sieger Design / D-Sassenberg		🔵			🟨		616	9
Tupperware / B-Aalst	🟠			🟣			592	10

Public Design/
Public Design

Firma / Ort	O	T	Y	P	G	R	Punkte	Rang
BEGA Gantenbrink-Leuchten / D-Menden	●	●		●	●		700	1
wiege Entwicklungsges. / D-Bad Münder		●		●	●	●	596	2
ECKE:Design / D-Berlin	●	●	●	●	●		538	3
Neumeister Design / D-München			●		●		418	4
Roy Fleetwood / GB-Cambridge			●			●	320	5
Knud Holscher Industriel Design / DK-Copenhagen		●			●		308	6
Bauwerkstatt Winkels / D-Dortmund				●	●		296	7
Grimshaw Industrial Design / GB-London	●			●	●		272	8
Burkhardt Leitner constructiv / D-Stuttgart			●	●			264	9
Leitner / D-Waiblingen			●			●	212	10

Freizeit, Sport und Spiel/
Leisure, Sports and Play

Firma / Ort	O	T	Y	P	G	R	Punkte	Rang
Cognito Design und Engineering / D-Oberhausen				●	●	●	692	1
BMW / D-München			●		●	●	676	2
Yamaha / J-Hamamatsu Shizuoka pref.		●		●	●		416	3
SRAM / D-Schweinfurt		●			●	●	396	4
yellow circle / D-Köln			●			●	378	5
Volkswagen / D-Wolfsburg		●				●	376	6
plus design / D-Köln	●	●					260	7
Deutsche Angelgeräte Manufaktur / D-Gunzenhausen		●		●			256	8
Storck Bicycle / D-Bad Camberg		●		●			216	9
Sonor Joh. Link Musikinstrumente / D-Bad Berleburg	●	●					200	10

Accessoires/
Accessoires

Firma / Ort	O	T	Y	P	G	R	Punkte	Rang
BREE Collection / D-Isernhagen	●	●	●	●	●	●	1380	1
Rodenstock / D-München	●	●			●		720	2
Gebr. Niessing / D-Vreden	●	●	●		●		647	3
Meister + Co. / CH-Wollerau	●	●			●		584	4
Peter Kövari / D-Pullach	●	●		●			420	5
Silhouette International Schmied / A-Linz				●	●	●	416	6
Samsonite Europe / B-Oudenaarde		●	●			●	408	7
Ferdinand Menrad / D-Krailing			●	●		●	384	8
deSIGN Markus T. / D-Gütersloh					●	●	368	9
Atelier Eva Katarina Bruggmann / CH-Zürich						●	208	10
Pur-Atelier für Schmuckgestaltung / D-Nettetal		●	●				208	10

Adressen Industrie-Design/

Addresses Industrial Design

AEG Hausgeräte GmbH
Muggenhofer Straße 135
90429 Nürnberg

Studio Ambrozus
Bismarckstraße 50
50672 Köln

Apple Computer GmbH
Dornacher Straße 3d
85622 Feldkirchen

Audi AG
Postfach
85045 Ingolstadt

Matthias Bader
Westbahnstraße 15
76829 Landau

BAHCO BELZER GmbH
Hastener Straße 4
42349 Wuppertal

BMW AG
80788 München
Seiten/*Pages* 34/35, 62/63, 100/101, 140/141

Robert Bosch Hausgeräte GmbH
Hochstraße 17
81669 München
Seiten/*Pages* 52/53, 122/123

BREE Collection GmbH & Co. KG
Gerberstraße 3
30916 Isernhagen

**Atelier
Eva Katharina Bruggmann**
Junghofstraße 16
CH-8050 Zürich

Canon Inc.
Europapark Fichtenhain A10
47807 Krefeld

**Cognito Design
und Engineering GmbH**
Sofienstraße 21
68794 Oberhausen-Rheinhausen

Crown Gabelstapler GmbH
Moosacher Straße 52
80809 München
Seiten/*Pages* 36/37

DaimlerChrysler AG
71059 Sindelfingen

designafairs GmbH
Tölzer Straße 2c
81379 München

**deSIGN
Markus T. GmbH**
Isselhorster Straße 374
33334 Gütersloh

Designworks/USA
Lothstraße 5
80335 München

Deutsche Bahn AG
Potsdamer Platz 2
10785 Berlin

designpraxis diener
Irisweg 3
89079 Ulm

einmaleins - Büro für Gestaltung
Im Weitblick 1
88483 Burgrieden

Ergonomi Design
Box 14 004
S-16714 Bromma

Festo AG & Co.
Rechbergstraße 3
73770 Denkendorf
Seiten/*Pages* 20/21, 74/75, 90/91, 154/155

Fiskars Consumer Oy AB
FIN-10330 Billnäs
Seiten/*Pages* 144/145

Fitch Inc. USA
10350 Olentangy River Road
USA-43085 Worthington, Ohio

Roy Fleetwood Ltd.
1 St. John's Innovation Park, Cowley Road
GB-CB4 4WS Cambridge

Foster and Partners
Riverside Three / 22 Hester Road
GB-SW11 4AN London

Ganymed GmbH
Breitenloh 7
82335 Berg/Starnberger See
Seiten/*Pages* 28/29

Carsten Gollnick
product design/interior design
Bülowstraße 66
10783 Berlin

Grimshaw Industrial Design
1 Conway Street, Fitzroy Sq.
GB-WIT 6LR London

Hawle Armaturen
Liegnitzer Straße 6
83395 Freilassing
Seiten/*Pages* 136/137

Heidebrecht Design
Büro für Produktplanung
Ensinger Straße 11
89073 Ulm

Heidelberger Druckmaschinen AG
Speyerer Straße 4
69115 Heidelberg

Held + Team
Schrammsweg 11
20249 Hamburg
Seiten/*Pages* 26/27

Henssler und Schultheiss
Fullservice Productdesign GmbH
Weissensteiner Straße 28
73525 Schwäbisch Gmünd

Rolf Hertkorn Design
Bahnhofstraße 11
88214 Ravensburg

Honda Motor Europe
(North) GmbH
Sprendlinger Landstraße 166
63069 Offenbach

IBM Deutschland GmbH
Am Fichtenberg 1
71083 Herrenberg

James Irvine
Via Sirtori 4
I-20129 Mailand

Jaguar Deutschland GmbH
Frankfurter Straße
61476 Kronberg

Jehs & Laub
Römerstraße 51a
70193 Stuttgart

Kienzledesign
Stickerinnenstraße 2
78467 Konstanz

Prof. Josef P. Kleihues
Fasanenstraße 26
10719 Berlin

Justus Kolberg,
Office for Industrial Design
Hochallee 106
20149 Hamburg

Korb + Korb
Schartenstraße 3
CH-5400 Baden

Leitner GmbH
Düsseldorfer Straße 14
71332 Waiblingen

Studio Arch. Michele de Lucchi
Via Pallavicino, 31
I-20145 Milano

MA Design
Duvelsbeker Weg 12
24105 Kiel

Erik Magnussen
620 Strandvejen
DK-2930 Klampenborg

Peter Maly
Oberstraße 46
20144 Hamburg

Ferdinand Menrad GmbH+Co.KG
Oderstraße 2
73522 Schwäbisch Gmünd

Micro Mobility Systems
Bahnhofstraße 10
CH-8700 Küsnacht
Seiten/*Pages* 64/65

Microsoft GmbH
Einsteinstraße 12
85716 Unterschleißheim

Miele & Cie. GmbH & Co.
Carl-Miele-Straße 29
33332 Gütersloh
Seiten/*Pages* 54/55, 130/131

Jasper Morrison Office for Design
5 Old Street
GB-EC 1V 9HL London

Pascal Mourgue
2, Rue Marcelin Berthelot
F-93100 Montreuil-Sous-Bois

Neumeister Design
Liebigstraße 8
80538 München

nlplk industrial design bv
Noordeinde 2d
NL-2311 CD Leiden

nya nordiska textiles gmbh
An den Ratswiesen
29451 Dannenberg
Seiten/*Pages* 42/43, 110/111

OLIGO Lichttechnik GmbH
Schlossstraße 7
53757 St. Augustin
Seiten/Pages 44/45

Phanos Gestaltung + Vertrieb GmbH
Osterdeich 7
28203 Bremen

Philips Design
Emmasingel 24
NL-5611 Eindhoven AZ

Phoenix Product Design
Kölner Straße 16
70376 Stuttgart
Seiten/Pages 70/71

arche design H. Piltz
Himmelsreichallee 51
48149 Münster

Pilotprojekt
Havichhorststraße 14-16
48145 Münster

piu products
Max-Keith-Straße 33
45136 Essen

Dr. Ing. h.c. F. Porsche AG
Porscheplatz 1
70435 Stuttgart

Proform Design
Seehalde 16
71364 Winnenden

Rokitta Produkt & Markenästhetik
Peutestraße 77
20539 Hamburg

Samsonite Europe N.V.
Westerring 17
B-9700 Oudenaarde

Samsung Electronics Co. Ltd.
Am Kronberger Hang 6
65824 Schwalbach / Taunus

Rainer Schindhelm Industrie-Design
Am Goldberg 8
94094 Rotthalmünster

Design Tech Jürgen R. Schmid
Zeppelinstraße 53
72119 Ammerbuch

Sedus Stoll AG
Brückenstraße 15
79761 Waldshut

Sharp Electronic (Europe) GmbH
Sonninstraße 3
20097 Hamburg

Sieger Design
Schloss Harkotten
48336 Sassenberg

Siemens-Electrogeräte GmbH
Hochstraße 17
81669 München
Seiten/Pages 48/49, 50/51, 116/117, 156/157

Silhouette International Schmied AG
Ellbognerstraße 24
A-4021 Linz

SNIKE Sport GmbH
Ludwigstraße 57
70176 Stuttgart

Sony Europe GmbH
Kemperplatz 1
10785 Berlin

SPECTRAL GESELLSCHAFT FÜR LICHTTECHNIK mbH
Bötzinger Straße 31
79111 Freiburg im Breisgau

SRAM Deutschland GmbH
Romstraße 1
97424 Schweinfurt

Philippe Starck
27, Rue Pierre Poli
F-92130 Issy les Moulineaux

Studiowerk Design
Forellenstraße 11
82266 Inning / Ammersee

Studio X
21 Powis Mews
GB-W11 1JN London

TEAMS Design GmbH
Kollwitzstraße 1
73728 Esslingen
Seiten/*Pages* 22/23

Designstudio Matteo Thun
Via Appiani 9
I-20121 Milano

Tools Design
Rentemestervej 23 a
DK-2400 Copenhagen
Seiten/*Pages* 56/57

Vistapark GmbH
Viehofstraße 119
42117 Wuppertal

Volkswagen AG
38436 Wolfsburg

Wall AG
Friedrichstraße 118
10117 Berlin

wiege Entwicklungsges.mbH
Hauptstraße 81
31848 Bad Münder

Wilkinson Sword
Schützenstraße 110
42659 Solingen

yellow circle
Georgstraße 5a
50676 Köln

Die 100 Besten / Hersteller
The Top 100 / Manufacturers

Handwerk und Industrie
Trade and Industry

Rang/*Rank*

Festo / D-Denkendorf / 1159 Punkte/*Points*	1
Heidelberger Druckmaschinen / D-Heidelberg / 456 Punkte/*Points*	2
Robert Bosch / D-München / 256 Punkte/*Points*	3
Metabowerke / D-Nürtingen / 192 Punkte/*Points*	4
Karl Dungs / D-Urbach / 184 Punkte/*Points*	5
BAHCO BELZER / D-Wuppertal / 144 Punkte/*Points*	6
Hilti / FL-Schaan / 144 Punkte/*Points*	6
Balzers Verschleißschutz / D-Bingen-Kempten / 128 Punkte/*Points*	8
C. & E. Fein / D-Stuttgart / 128 Punkte/*Points*	8
Ferag / CH-Hinwil / 128 Punkte/*Points*	8
Alfred Kärcher / D-Winnenden / 128 Punkte/*Points*	8
Multi-Contact / D-Essen / 128 Punkte/*Points*	8
Georg Schlegel / D-Dürmentingen / 128 Punkte/*Points*	8
SMC Corporation / D-Egelsbach / 128 Punkte/*Points*	8
Vollmer Werke / D-Biberach / 128 Punkte/Points	8
MIWE Michael Wenz / D-Arnstein / 128 Punkte/Points	8

Festo AG & Co. KG
Corporate Design

Anschrift/*Address*
Rechbergstraße 3
D-73770 Denkendorf
Ansprechpartner/*Contact*
Prof. Dipl.-Ing. Axel Thallemer
Head of Corporate Design
Telefon/*Phone*
+49(0)711/3 47 38 80
Telefax/*Fax*
+49(0)711/3 47 38 99
E-mail/*E-mail*
tem@festo.com

Handwerk und Industrie / *Trade and Industry*

Festo 1

Georg Schlegel GmbH & Co.

Anschrift/*Address*
Am Kapellenweg
D-88525 Dürmentingen

Ansprechpartner/*Contact*
Herr Geisinger und Herr Zoll

Telefon/*Phone*
+49 (0)7371/ 502-0

Telefax/*Fax*
+49 (0)7371/ 502-49

E-mail/*E-mail*
info@schlegel.biz

Internet/*Website*
www.schlegel.biz

Gründungsdatum/*Foundation*
1945

Mitarbeiter/*Employees*
140

Filiale/*Branch Office*
in über 50 Ländern
In more than 50 countries

Design/*Design*
Prof. Horst Diener

Tätigkeitsfelder/*Fields of Activity*
Herstellung von Befehlsgeräten, Reihenklemmen, Fußschaltern, Meldeleuchten, Folien- und Kurzhubtastaturen, Gehäusen, Endschaltern, Bedientableaus, Funktionsbausteinen
Production of control units, terminal blocks, pedal switches, pilot lights, membrane and short-travel keyboards, enclosures, limit switches, panels, functional modules

Die Befehlsgeräte der Firma Georg Schlegel GmbH & Co. finden überwiegend ihren Einsatz in Bedientableaus von Maschinen und Geräten. Design spielt beim Bau von Maschinen eine zunehmend wichtigere Rolle und so stellen Befehlsgeräte ein ideales "Design-Bindeglied" zwischen Bedienung einerseits und Maschinenfunktion andererseits dar. Dabei zeichnen sich die Schlegel Befehlsgeräte-Baureihen durch hohe Funktionalität, Ergonomie und exzellente Qualität und eben auch durch ihr eigenständiges Design aus. Zahlreiche Designauszeichnungen, bis heute über 60 nationale und internationale Auszeichnungen, bestätigen die Richtigkeit dieses Konzeptes. Innovatives Design und höchste Qualität sind somit die wichtigsten Produkteigenschaften von Befehlsgeräten der Firma Georg Schlegel GmbH & Co.

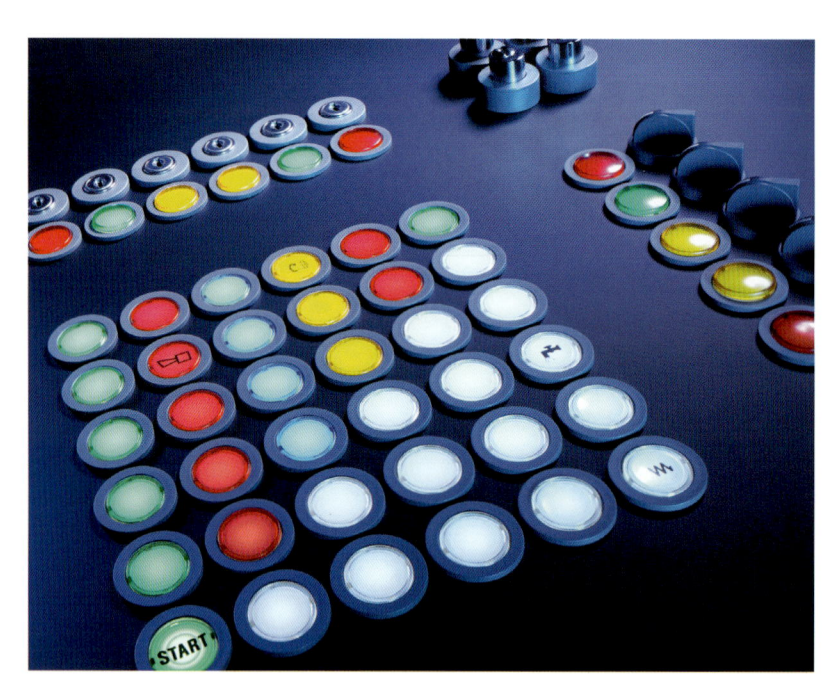

Befehlsgeräte Baureihe RX-JUWEL, Schutzart IP65
Control Units series RX-JUWEL, protection type IP65

Not-Aus-Taste Baureihe RX-JUWEL
Emergency-off pushbutton series RX-JUWEL

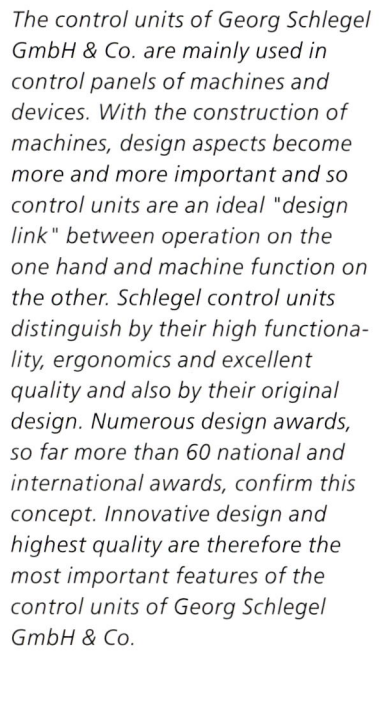

The control units of Georg Schlegel GmbH & Co. are mainly used in control panels of machines and devices. With the construction of machines, design aspects become more and more important and so control units are an ideal "design link" between operation on the one hand and machine function on the other. Schlegel control units distinguish by their high functionality, ergonomics and excellent quality and also by their original design. Numerous design awards, so far more than 60 national and international awards, confirm this concept. Innovative design and highest quality are therefore the most important features of the control units of Georg Schlegel GmbH & Co.

Not-Aus-Taste mit 9 mm Einbautiefe für Flacheingabesysteme
Emergency-off pushbutton with 9 mm mounting depth for flat-input keyboards

Befehlsgeräte für exklusive Anwendungen aus Edelstahl Baureihe RVA, Schutzart IP65
Control Units for exclusive applications made of special steel series RVA, protection type IP65

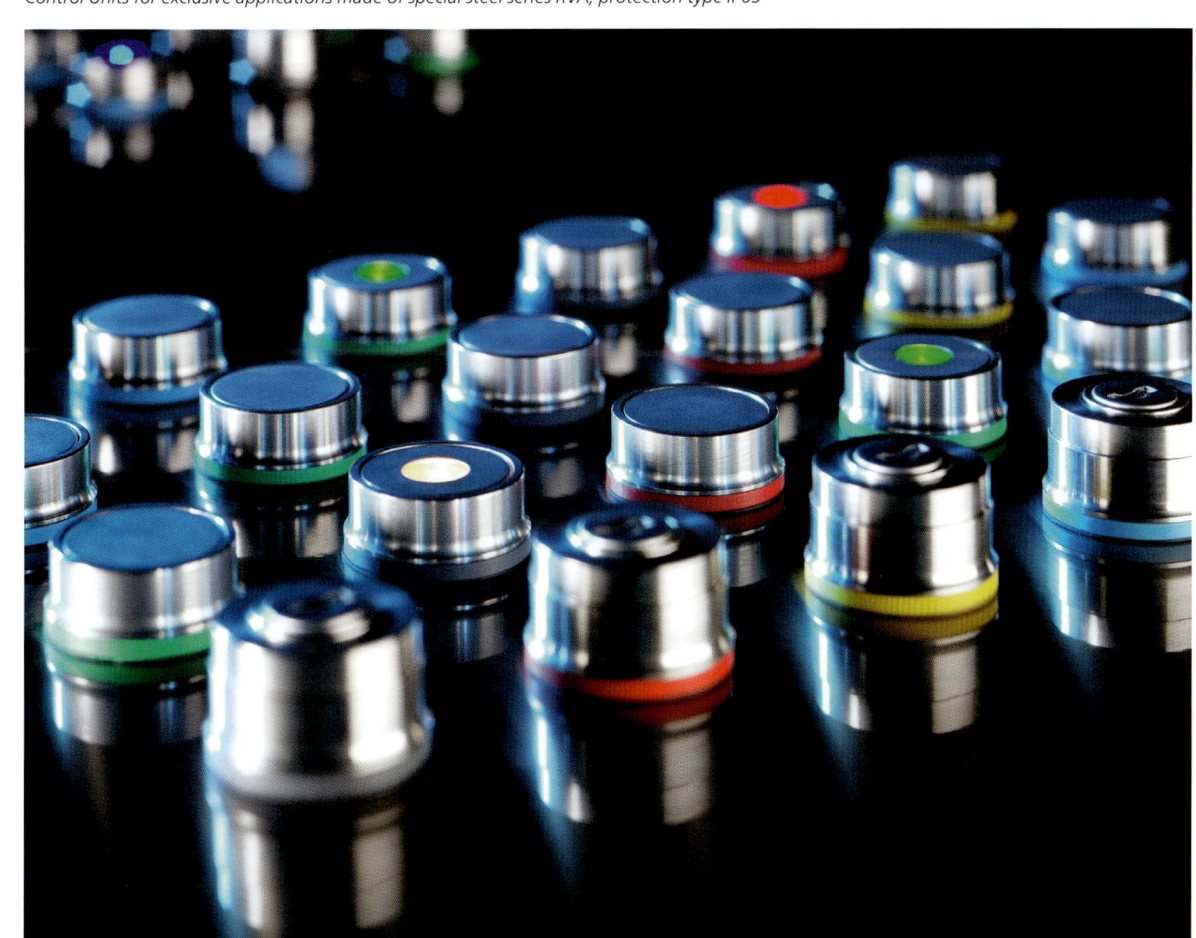

Medizin und Rehabilitation
Medicine and Rehabilitation

Rang/*Rank*

Siemens / D-München / 200 Punkte/*Points*	1
Thermamed / D-Bad Oeynhausen / 192 Punkte/*Points*	2
Ulrich Alber / D-Albstadt / 170 Punkte/*Points*	3
Bauerfeind Orthopädie / D-Kempen / 150 Punkte/*Points*	4
Paul Hartmann / D-Heidenheim / 144 Punkte/*Points*	5
Ganymed / D-Berg / 132 Punkte/*Points*	6
Olympus Winter & Ibe / D-Hamburg / 128 Punkte/*Points*	7
Pharmacia / D-Erlangen / 128 Punkte/*Points*	7
Renfert / D-Hilzingen / 128 Punkte/*Points*	7
Sirona Dental Systems / D-Bensheim / 128 Punkte/*Points*	7

Medien, Kommunikation und Unterhaltungselektronik
Media, Communication and Entertainment Electronics

	Rang/*Rank*
IBM / D-Herrenberg / 1424 Punkte/*Points*	1
Sony Europe / D-Berlin / 1376 Punkte/*Points*	2
Samsung Electronics / D-Schwalbach / 712 Punkte/*Points*	3
Loewe Opta / D-Kronach / 526 Punkte/*Points*	4
Canon / D-Krefeld / 512 Punkte/*Points*	5
Apple Computer / D-Feldkirchen / 400 Punkte/*Points*	6
Sharp Electronic / D-Hamburg / 392 Punkte/*Points*	7
Microsoft / D-Unterschleißheim / 320 Punkte/*Points*	8
Philips / NL-Eindhoven / 320 Punkte/*Points*	8
Iomega / CH-Petit-Laney / 192 Punkte/*Points*	10
Matsushita / GB-Thatchham / 192 Punkte/*Points*	10
Siemens / D-München / 192 Punkte/*Points*	10

Verkehrsmittel und Sonderfahrzeuge
Transportation and Special Use Vehicles

	Rang/*Rank*
BMW / D-München / 548 Punkte/*Points*	1
Siemens DUEWAG / D-Krefeld / 294 Punkte/*Points*	2
Crown Gabelstapler / D-München / 256 Punkte/*Points*	3
DaimlerChrysler / D-Sindelfingen / 206 Punkte/*Points*	4
Bombardier Transportation / D-Berlin / 192 Punkte/*Points*	5
Dr. Ing. h.c. F. Porsche / D-Stuttgart / 192 Punkte/*Points*	5
Audi / D-Ingolstadt / 178 Punkte/*Points*	7
Honda / D-Offenbach / 144 Punkte/*Points*	8
Jaguar / D-Kronberg / 144 Punkte/*Points*	8
British Airways / GB-Harmondsworth / 128 Punkte/*Points*	10
Hankook Reifen / D-Dreieich / 128 Punkte/*Points*	10
Still / D-Hamburg / 128 Punkte/*Points*	10

BMW AG

Anschrift/*Address*
D-80788 München

Ansprechpartner/*Contact*
Abteilung Öffentlichkeitsarbeit
Public Relation Department

Telefon/*Phone*
+49 (0)89/38 20

Internet/*Website*
www.BMWgroup.de

Der Designprozess der BMW Group gewährleistet die hohe Emotionalität der Produkte vom Zeitpunkt der Vision bis zur Erscheinung als charaktervolle Persönlichkeiten auf den Straßen. Das Spannungsfeld zwischen Emotion und Rationalität, zwischen Leidenschaft für Technologie und Design lässt jene Skulpturen in einem einzigartigen Prozess entstehen.

The design process of the BMW Group implements high emotion into products, from the moment of the designer's vision up to their appearance as personalities on the streets. These sculptures are born in a unique process of tension between emotion and rationality, between passion for technology and design.

Verkehrsmittel und Sonderfahrzeuge/Transportation and special use vehicles

BMW

Büro und Objekt
Office and Public Space

	Rang/Rank
Sedus Stoll / D-Waldshut / 448 Punkte/*Points*	1
SPECTRAL GESELLSCHAFT FÜR LICHTTECHNIK / D-Freiburg / 400 Punkte/*Points*	2
Gebrüder Thonet / D-Frankenberg / 400 Punkte/*Points*	2
iGuzzini / D-Planegg / 320 Punkte/*Points*	4
Vitra / D-Weil am Rhein / 275 Punkte/*Points*	5
MABEG Kreuschner / D-Soest / 272 Punkte/*Points*	6
Fritz Hansen / DK-Allerød / 208 Punkte/*Points*	7
Unifor / I-Turate / 192 Punkte/*Points*	8
Wilkhahn Wilkening + Hahne / D-Bad Münder / 192 Punkte/*Points*	8
Carpet Concept Objekt-Teppichboden / D-Bielefeld / 184 Punkte/*Points*	10

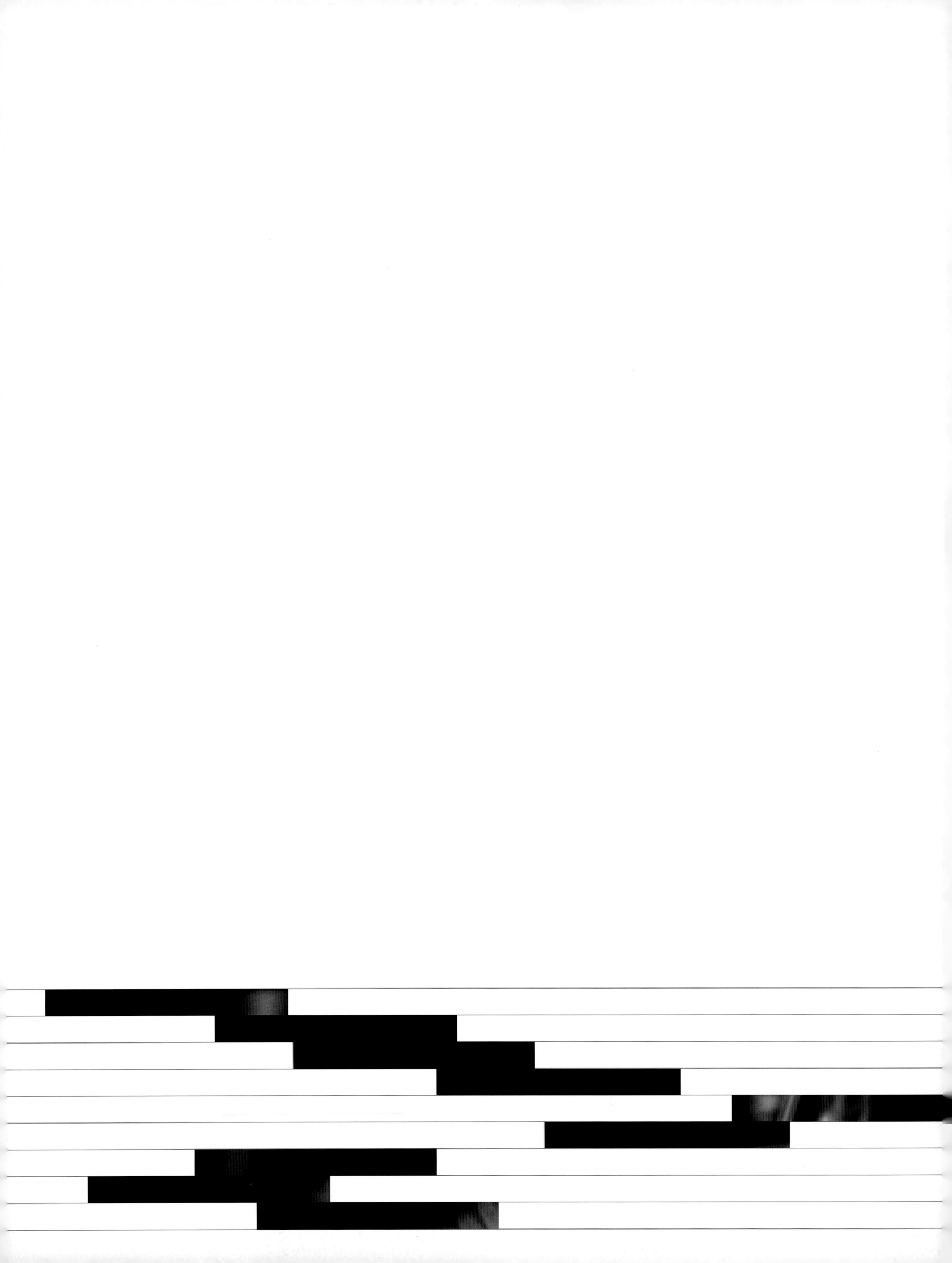

Wohnung
Living

	Rang/*Rank*
Gira Giersiepen / D-Radevormwald / 493 Punkte/*Points*	1
Artemide / D-Fröndenberg / 297 Punkte/*Points*	2
nya nordiska / D-Dannenberg / 256 Punkte/*Points*	3
ClassiCon / D-München / 208 Punkte/*Points*	4
interlübke Gebr. Lübke / D-Rheda-Wiedenbrück / 128 Punkte/*Points*	5
Merten / D-Wiehl / 128 Punkte/*Points*	5
Moormann Möbel / D-Aschau / 128 Punkte/*Points*	5
Phanos / D-Bremen / 128 Punkte/*Points*	5
Roset / D-Gundelfingen / 128 Punkte/*Points*	5
Schmitz-Werke / D-Emsdetten / 128 Punkte/*Points*	5

Gira Giersiepen GmbH & Co. KG

Anschrift/*Address*
Postfach/*P.O. Box 12 20*
D-42461 Radevormwald
Dahlienstraße
D-42477 Radevormwald
Telefon/*Phone*
+49 (0)2195/602-0
Telefax/*Fax*
+49 (0)2195/602-339
+49 (0)2195/602-119 (Export)
E-mail/*E-mail*
info@gira.de
Internet/*Website*
www.gira.de
www.gira.com
Gründungsdatum/*Foundation*
1905
Mitarbeiter/*Employees*
750
Tätigkeitsfelder/*Fields of Activity*
Elektrotechnische Industrie
Electrotechnical industry

Einfach elektrisierend.

Moderne Elektroinstallation von Gira steht für intelligente, zukunftsorientierte Technik und flexible Lösungen verbunden mit hoher Designqualität.

Dabei gewinnt die Zusammenführung unterschiedlichster Bereiche zunehmend an Bedeutung: Immer neue Technologien wachsen über die Gira Designplattformen mit der Elektroinstallation zusammen und werden Bestandteil der Schalterwelt. Seit langem erfolgreich integriert sind z. B. Netzwerktechnik und Telekommunikations-Anschlüsse sowie Funktionen für Bustechnologien. 2003 nun holt Gira die Türkommunikationstechnik in die Schalterwelt – und rundet auch das Rauchmelder- und Alarmsystem-Sortiment weiter ab.

Entwickelt werden die Produkte in enger Zusammenarbeit mit externen und hausinternen Designteams, dem Elektro-Fachvertrieb sowie Planern und Architekten.

Mehr über Gira und die Gira Produkte erfahren Sie im Internet unter: www.gira.de.

Gira Wohnungsstation Komfort mit Hörer aus dem Gira Türkommunikations-System. Ausgezeichnet mit dem „Design Plus".
Gira indoor station comfort with handset from the Gira door communication system. Awarded the „Design Plus" award.

Gira Rauchmelder/VdS.
Von der Stiftung Warentest
getestet und für gut befunden.
Ausgezeichnet mit dem red dot
und if Product Design award.
Gira smoke detector/VdS.
Tested and approved by the
German consumer test institute
(Stiftung Warentest).
Awarded the „red dot" and
„if Product Design" awards.

Gira Esprit.
Schalterprogramm mit Rahmen aus
Echtmaterialien, einfach und edel.
Ausgezeichnet mit dem Roten Punkt
für Hohe Designqualität und dem
„Design Plus".
Gira Esprit. Design range with
frames made of genuine materials
simple and noble.
Awarded with the „red dot"
award for high design quality and
the „Design Plus" award.

Gira Tastsensor 2.
Für komfortables Steuern, Schalten
und Dimmen in Verbindung
mit den Gira Bussystemen.
Mit hinterleuchtetem Beschriftungs-
feld. Ausgezeichnet mit dem
„Design Plus".
Gira push button sensor 2.
For comfortable controlling,
switching and dimming in
combination with the Gira bus
systems. With back-lit labeled
surface. Awarded the „Design Plus"
award.

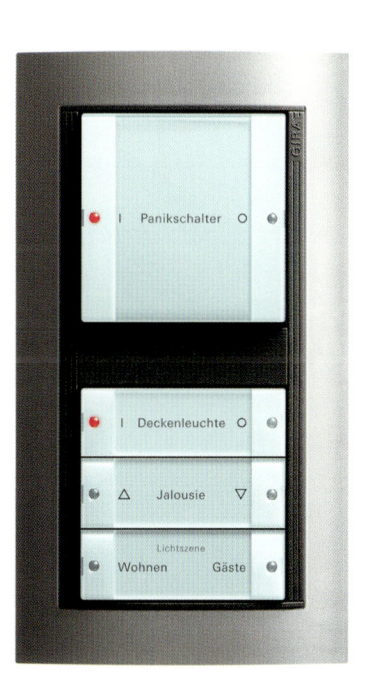

Simply electrifying.

Modern electrical installations of
Gira stands for intelligent future-
oriented technology and flexible
solutions combined with high
design quality.

The combination of various ranges
is increasing in importance:
More and more new technologies
have fused through the Gira design
platforms with the electrical
installation and become part of the
world of switches. Network
technology and telecommunication
connections as well as functions
for bus technologies have, for
example, been integrated success-
fully. In 2003 Gira is now integra-
ting the door communication
technology into the world of
switches – and is also rounding
off the smoke-detector and alarm-
system product assortment further.

The products are developed in
close cooperation with external
and in-house design teams, the
specialist electrical trade as well
as architects and planners.

Further information on Gira and
the Gira products can be obtained
in the Internet under:
www.gira.com

Artemide GmbH

Anschrift/Address
Hans-Böckler-Straße 2
D-58730 Fröndenberg
Telefon/Phone
+49 (0)2373/9 75-0
Telefax/Fax
+49 (0)2373/9 75-224
E-mail/E-mail
ml@artemide.de
Internet/Website
www.artemide.com
Gründungsdatum/Foundation
1959 durch Ernesto Gismondi
Filialen/Branch Offices
15 Konzerngesellschaften,
Exklusivverkaufsstellen in
47 Ländern, Werke in Italien,
Frankreich, Deutschland, Ungarn,
USA und der Tschechei
*15 associated companies,
exclusive sales offices in
47 countries, factories in Italy,
France, Germany, Hungary,
USA and the Czech Republic*
Mitarbeiter/Employees
70
Kunden/Clients
Architekten, Lichtplaner,
Ingenieurbüros und
Facheinzelhandel
*Architects, light planners,
engineer's offices and retail trade*
Tätigkeitsfelder/Fields of Activity
Design, Planung und Produktion
von Leuchten
*Design, planning and production
of luminaires*

Als designorientiertes Unternehmen bietet Artemide ein umfangreiches Programm technischer und dekorativer Leuchten von namhaften internationalen Designern, wie z. B. Mario Botta, Sir Norman Foster, Michele De Lucchi, Richard Sapper, Ettore Sottsass u.v.m.

Dabei konzentriert sich Artemide auf die Planung von Leuchten, welche die perfekte Synthese von Design, Funktion, Innovation und Effizienz darstellen.

Somit arbeitet Artemide für eine Kombination von Design und Technik, die sich ganz dem Wohlbefinden des Menschen unterordnet. In einem konstanten Entwicklungsprozess setzt Artemide ständig neue, zukunftsweisende Akzente im Designbereich.

Die Produktlinien der Artemide-Gruppe umfassen: Artemide, Metamorfosi, Collezioni, Architectural Indoor & Outdoor und Modern Classic. Jede Produktlinie ist stilistisch klar ausgeprägt und entspricht damit den unterschiedlichen Bedürfnissen der Zielgruppen.

Viele Artemide Leuchten sind bereits mit nationalen und internationalen Auszeichnungen geehrt worden.

SUI Design: Carlotta de Bevilacqua - 2001
Farben: Metallic-Blau, Metallic-Bronze,
Leuchtmittel: 18 x LED Weiß
Material: Polykarbonat,
Maße: cm 8 (B) x 23 (L) x 24 (H)
LED-Tischleuchte, die durch eine leichte Berührung (Microswitch) einzuschalten ist. Durch ihre handgerechte Form und den möglichen Akkubetrieb ist SUI auch als Taschenlampe zu verwenden. Eine farbige LED in der abgerundeten Basis zeigt den jeweiligen Ladezustand des Akkus an. Direkte Lichtverteilung.

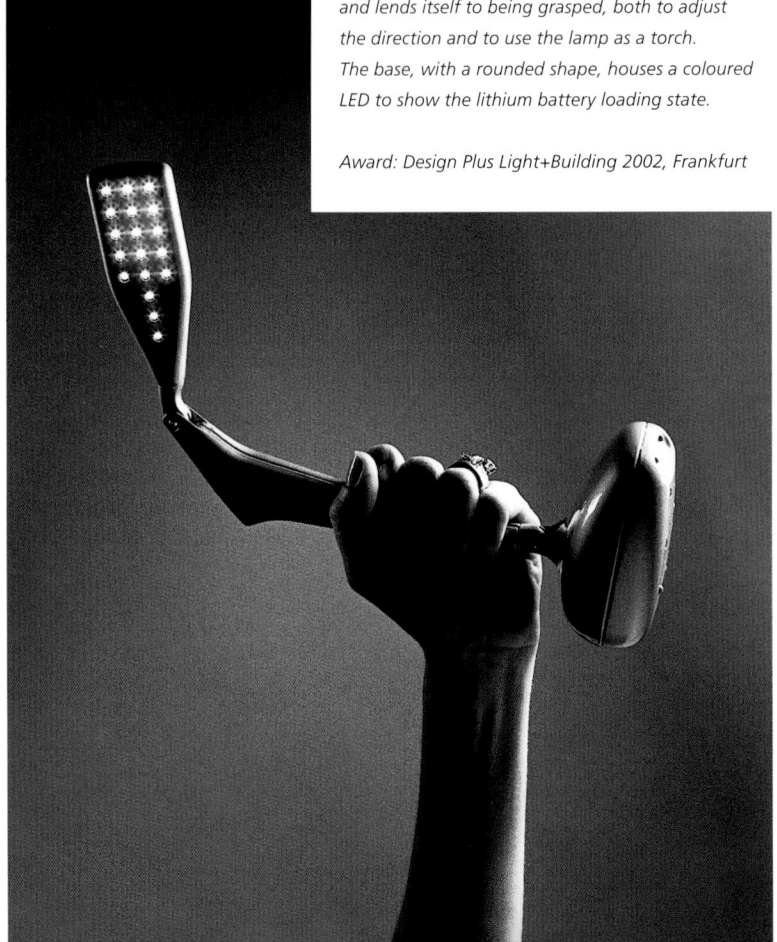

*Colours: Metallic blue, metallic bronze
Material: Polycarbonate
Rechargeable portable task-lamp. The polycarbonate body houses an on/off touch device (microswitch) and lends itself to being grasped, both to adjust the direction and to use the lamp as a torch. The base, with a rounded shape, houses a coloured LED to show the lithium battery loading state.*

Award: Design Plus Light+Building 2002, Frankfurt

IERACE Design: Matali Crasset - 2001
Farben: Silbergrau und Transparent
Material: Rahmen aus lackiertem Metall, Rosette aus lackiertem Polykarbonat, äußerer Lichtverteiler aus transparentem Glas, zwei innere Lichtverteiler aus Polykarbonat
Die Kabel zur Deckenaufhängung der Leuchte unterstreichen den optisch leichten Eindruck des Designs und dienen gleichzeitig als Netzkabel.

Colours: Silver grey and transparent
Material: Painted aluminium structure and polycarbonate rose. Transparent blown glass external diffuser, two polycarbonate internal diffusers.
As well as making the form of the lamp light, the four suspension cables also supply the power. Direct and indirect light emission.
Awards: Prix L'Observer du Design 2002, Paris, Baden-Württemberg International Design Award 2001

As a design-oriented company, Artemide presents an extensive programme of technical and decorative lamps from famous international designers like Mario Botta, Sir Norman Foster, Michele De Lucchi, Richard Sapper, Ettore Sottass etc.

It is very important for Artemide to create and project lamps, which represent the perfect synthesis of design, function, innovation and efficiency.

TALO SYSTEM Design: Neil Poulton – 2001, 2002
Farben: Weiß oder Silbergrau
Material: Rosette aus Kunststoff, Körper aus lackiertem Aluminium, oberer Schirm aus transparentem Polykarbonat, unterer Schirm aus Polykarbonat.
Die Produktreihe TALO besteht aus Wand- und Hängeleuchten in unterschiedlichen Ausführungen und Abmessungen.
Ihre stromlinienförmige Eleganz ergänzt sich optimal mit verschiedenen Stilrichtungen und Umgebungen, im Büro oder zu Hause. Dabei ermöglicht der Einsatz von Leuchtstoffröhren einen minimalen Stromverbrauch und optimalen Lichtfluss. Direkte und indirekte Lichtverteilung.

Colours: White or silver grey
Material: Thermoplastic resin rose. Painted aluminium body, transparent polycarbonate upper diffuser, polycarbonate lower diffuser.
TALO is a series of lamps for wall and suspension mounting in various lengths. The streamlined elegance of the luminaire blends into any decor, commercial or domestic. High power fluorescent tubes guarantee major energy savings and greater light flow. Direct and indirect light emission.

Awards: reddot award 2002, Essen, iF design award 2002, Hannover, Prix L'Observer du Design 2002, Paris

In this way Artemide works for a combination of technology and design, which is submitted to human comfort and health.
In a permanent process of development Artemide constantly composes new accents and aspects, which are very important for the future of product design.

The product lines of the Artemide group are: Artemide, Metamorfosi, Collezioni, Architectural Indoor & Outdoor and Modern Classic.
Each product line has its typical clear character and style and satisfies the different and individual demands of the target groups.

Many lamps of Artemide are honored with national and international design awards.

LOGICO SYSTEM Design: Michele De Lucchi, Gerhard Reichert – 2001, 2002
Farbe: Aluminiumgrau
Material: Rahmen aus lackiertem Metall, Lichtverteiler aus mundgeblasenem Opalglas mit Endstück aus glänzender Seide.
Die LOGICO Produktlinie besteht aus Tisch-, Steh-, Decken- und Hängeleuchten und wurde aus der Idee geboren, Beleuchtungssysteme von Grund auf zu erneuern - angefangen bei der Technik und der Methode der Lichtdiffusion. Der raffinierte Schirm aus mundgeblasenem Glas ist in verschiedenen Versionen erhältlich. Dabei gestattet es seine organische Form, vielerlei unterschiedliche Kompositionen zu schaffen, die mannigfaltige Licht- und Formgestalten ins Leben rufen können.

Color: Aluminium grey
Material: Painted metal structure, blown glass opal diffuser with finish in polished silk.
LOGICO is available in table, ceiling, suspension and floor versions and in two sizes. The series was originated from an idea of organizing a system based on light diffusion. The sophisticated blown glass diffuser is used in different versions. Its organic and sinuous form lends itself to the creation of multiple combinators.

Awards: reddot award 2002, Essen, iF design award 2002, Hannover

nya nordiska

Anschrift/*Address*
An den Ratswiesen
D-29451 Dannenberg

Ansprechpartner/*Contact*
Bernhard Hansl

Telefon/*Phone*
+49 (0)5861/809-43

Telefax/*Fax*
+49 (0)5861/809-12

E-mail/*E-mail*
nya@nya.com

Internet/*Website*
www.nya.com

Gründungsdatum/*Foundation*
1964

Mitarbeiter/*Employees*
circa 100

Filiale/*Branch Office*
Como, Paris, London, Tokio

Tätigkeitsfelder/*Fields of Activity*
Produktentwicklung und Vertrieb von Heimtextilien
Product development and distribution of home textiles

ROSETTA

Hauchfeine, matte Garne sind Grundlage des einen, mittelfeine, mit Körper und Glanz, die des anderen Gewebes, beide vereint durch Bindungspunkte zum Doppelgewebe. Es bildet sich dabei ein dezenter, attraktiver Moiré.

Nach Aufspannen in einen Groß-Stickautomaten (Länge x Höhe = 15 x 5 Meter) wird dieses Gewebe mit farbigem Garn bestickt. Mitten in die grafischen Motive hinein werden Glas-Diamanten „geschossen". Das ist die Reihenfolge.

Bei allem - nichts ist überfrachtet. Die Kreation besticht in ihrer Schlichtheit.

An extremely fine, pale yarn is the basis of one, and a medium yarn, glossy and with more body, the basis of another fabric. The two materials are put together, by means of small, stitched dots, to create a double material. A discreet, attractive moiré is the result.

The material is stentered on a very large embroidery machine (length x height = 15 x 5 meters) and embroidered with a colored yarn. A rhinestone is "shot" in the center of the motifs. That is the sequence.

All in all, nothing is exaggerated. The creation impresses by it's sheer simplicity.

COLINI

Kettfäden, kaum wahrnehmbar, wie ein Hauch, dabei fest und dehnungsstabil, verbinden sich in perfekter Dreher-Technik mit diversen, teilweise wolligen, Effekt-Schüssen zu einem luftigen Etwas und geben freier, kreativer Gestaltung großen Spielraum.

Warp threads, like a breeze of air, hardly noticeable but still strong and stretchable. In a perfect spinning technique they combine themselves with various, sometimes woolly effect picks to a vivacious and airy something, allowing independent and creative designing.

Schmitz-Werke GmbH + Co. KG

Anschrift/Address
Hansestraße 87
D-48282 Emsdetten
Telefon/Phone
+49 (0)2572/972-0
Telefax/Fax
+49 (0)2572/92 74 44
E-mail/E-mail
info@schmitz-werke.com
Internet/Website
www.schmitz-werke.com
Gründungsdatum/Foundation
1921
Filialen/Branch Offices
Shanghai, England, Italien,
Frankreich, Niederlande
*Shanghai, England, Italy, France,
Netherlands*
Umsatz/Turnover
106 Mio. Euro (Gruppe)
106 million Euro (Group)
Mitarbeiter/Employees
885 (in 2002)
Kunden/Clients
Weltweite Kundschaft aus den
Bereichen Handel, Verleger im
Textilbereich, Architekten,
Objektteure, Raumausstatter,
Fachbetriebe der Metall-
verarbeitung, Schiffsausstatter,
Sonnenschutzhersteller,
Bootsbauer
*International clientele in the
trade sector, distributors in the
textiles branch, architects, flooring
and ceiling installers, interior
decorators, plants specialized in
metal processing, ship's chandlers,
UV protection manufacturers,
and boat builders.*
Tätigkeitsfelder/Fields of Activity
Hersteller von marilux-Markisen,
swela Gartenmöbelstoffen und
Freilufttextilien bzw. Outdoor-
stoffen sowie von drapilux
Dekorationsstoffen und Gardinen
*Manufacturer of marilux awnings,
swela garden furniture fabrics as
well as outdoors textiles, drapilux
decorative fabrics and draperies.*

Die Geschichte der Schmitz-Werke bietet jede Menge Stoff, ebenso über Qualität und Solidität zu sprechen, wie über Individualität und Kreativität. Anfangen hat alles mit der Gründung der „Emsdettener Baumwollindustrie", die seit ihrer Gründung in Jahre 1921 bereits erstklassigen Stoff für viele fortschrittliche Produktideen lieferte. Seither hat sich viel getan. Die Märkte sind größer und härter geworden, Kunden immer anspruchsvoller, und unsere Mittel und Wege ihnen gerecht zu werden, sind moderner und leistungsfähiger denn je.
Eines jedoch hat sich nicht geändert: Unsere konsequente qualitäts- und kundenorientierte Unternehmensphilosophie und unser Gefühl für meisterhaftes Handwerk. Diese einzigartige Verbindung von Hightech-Produktion und lebendiger Tradition macht uns zu einem starken Partner für den Handel und verarbeitende Unternehmen.

Unsere Dekorationsstoffe, Möbelstoffe, Freilufttextilien und kompletten Sonnenschutzanlagen und Beschattungssysteme gehen um die Welt. Dafür sorgt unser weltweites Vertriebsnetz mit Tochtergesellschaften und Verkaufsbüros/Werksvertretungen. Immer mit dabei: ein weit gefächertes Servicespektrum, mit dem wir unseren Partnern in aller Welt zur Seite stehen und das - perfekt abgestimmt auf unserem Produktionsspektrum – eine erfolgreiche Basis für eine erfolgreiche Zusammenarbeit bietet.

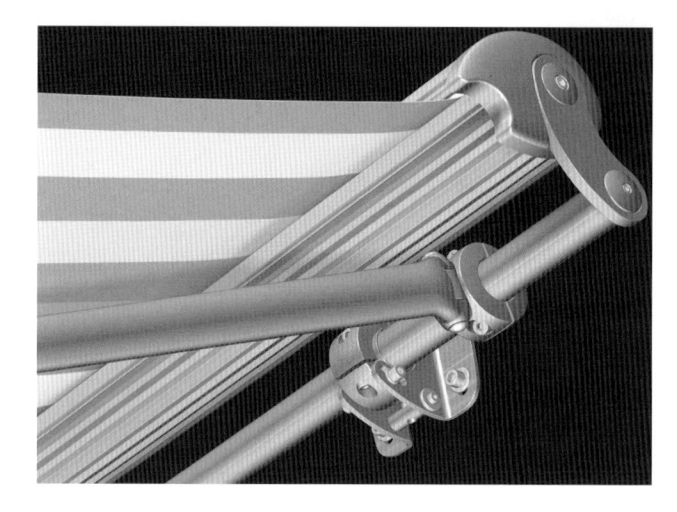

Diese Markise ist eine neue Markise. Sie ist Kunstwerk und Meisterstück. Meisterwerk und Kunststück. Die vollendete Verbindung von Form und Funktion und Material.

Die markilux ES-1 ist einzigartig. Aus seewasserfestem V4A-Edelstahl gefertigt. Mit modernster Technik für Ansprüche von heute. In einer Qualität wie für die Ewigkeit.

Ihre Gasdruckfedern bringen in jeder Phase Spannung in das Tuch. Ihr serienmäßiger Elektroantrieb treibt den Komfort auf die Spitze. Ihre Gelenkarme lagern nahezu zeitlos reibungslos in teflonbeschichteten Bronzebuchsen. Ihre seidenmatt gebürstete Oberfläche zeigt Wind und Wetter die kühle Schulter. Bis in die kleinste Schraube.

Die neue markilux ES-1 lässt Sinne wandeln. Und Körper sprechen. Man muss sie nicht haben. Die markilux ES-1 will man haben. Aus Leidenschaft. Aus Lust.

This awning is a novel awning. It is a work of art and a masterpiece. It is the work of a master and a work of art. The perfect union of form and function and matter.

The markilux ES-1 is unique. Made of sea water resistant V4A stainless steel. Equipped with the latest technology for today's demands. With quality designed for eternity.

The gas pistons tension the fabric in any phase. The standard electrical drive takes comfort to the top. The articulated arms glide in Teflon-coated gunmetal bushings, almost timelessly and without friction. The matt-brushed surface gives wind and weather the cold shoulder – right down to the smallest screw.

The novel markilux ES-1 takes your senses on a journey. And it makes bodies talk. You do not need it, but you want to have it. It is a matter of passion. And desire.

The history of Schmitz-Werke offers a large amount of material to speak about, as much about quality and sturdiness as about individuality and creativity. It all began with the foundation of the „Emsdetten Cotton Industry," which has delivered first class material for many progressive product ideas since its establishment in the year 1921. Much has happened since then. The market has gotten larger but also more complex, customers have become more demanding and in order to live up to these demands we have adjusted our ways and means to become more modern and more efficient than ever. One thing, however, remains unchanged: Our consistent quality, customer-oriented company philosophy and our feeling for masterful workmanship. Our unique combination of high-tech production and traditional quality makes us a strong partner for the trade and the processing industry.

Our decorative fabrics, upholstery materials, outdoor textiles, and sun protection and shading systems are conquering the world market. Our global distribution network of subsidiary branches, sales offices and sales representatives takes care of it. Always present: our wide and diverse spectrum of services; we are ready to come to the aid of all our partners worldwide, offering a winning basis for working together successfully and in perfect harmony with our range of products.

Haushalt, Küche und Bad
Household, Kitchen and Bath

	Rang/*Rank*
Siemens-Electrogeräte / D-München / 896 Punkte/*Points*	1
Viessmann Werke / D-Allendorf / 554 Punkte/*Points*	2
imperial-Werke / D-Bünde / 464 Punkte/*Points*	3
Hansgrohe / D-Schiltach / 376 Punkte/*Points*	4
Robert Bosch Hausgeräte / D-München / 362 Punkte/*Points*	5
WMF / D-Geislingen / 296 Punkte/*Points*	6
Hoesch Metall + Kunststoffwerk / D-Düren / 268 Punkte/*Points*	7
EVA / D-Moorrege / 256 Punkte/*Points*	8
alfi Zitzmann / D-Wertheim / 256 Punkte/*Points*	8
AEG Hausgeräte / D-Nürnberg / 192 Punkte/*Points*	10
Leonardo-glaskoch / D-Bad Driburg / 192 Punkte/*Points*	10
Miele & Cie. / D-Gütersloh / 192 Punkte/*Points*	10

Siemens-Electrogeräte GmbH
Designabteilung (MDS)

Anschrift/*Address*
Postfach 10 02 50
D-80076 München
Ansprechpartner/*Contact*
Gerd E. Wilsdorf
Telefon/*Phone*
+49 (0)89/45 90-32 35
Telefax/*Fax*
+49 (0)89/45 90-298
Mitarbeiter/*Employees*
12

Anspruchsvolle Technik und höchst sensible Sensorik übernehmen bei Siemens Geräten eine Vielzahl von Funktionen und sorgen so für entscheidend mehr Komfort. Funktionalität, die durch ihre Optik besticht, zeigt zum Beispiel die Sensorbedienung, die ganz ohne Knöpfe und Schalter auskommt. Oder das Dialog-Display bei der Waschmaschine serie IQ, bei der man über das Menü einfach das gewünschte Programm wählt, sowie die vollautomatische Programmwahl im Klartext-Display beim Geschirrspüler HiSense, das in die Tür-Oberkante integriert ist. Details, die dazu beitragen, den unverwechselbaren Charakter von Siemens Geräten zu prägen.

Glaskeramik-Kochfeld mit Digitalanzeige
Glass-ceramic hob with digital display

Waschmaschine serie IQ mit Dialog-Display
serie IQ washing machine with dialogue display
WIQ 1630
Design J. Geyer, Gerd E. Wilsdorf

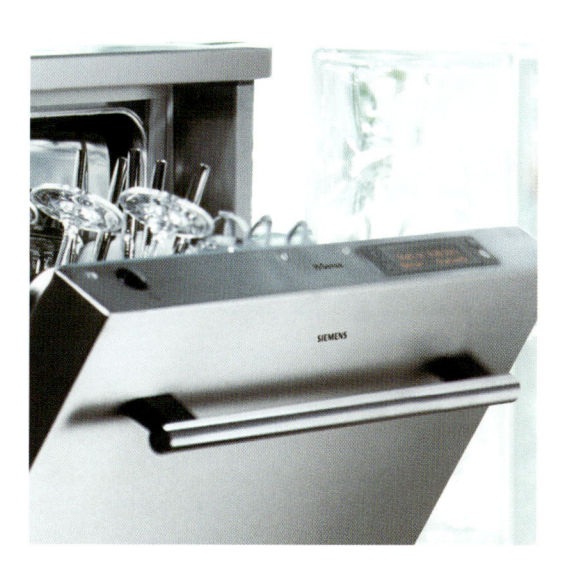

Geschirrspüler HiSense mit Klartext-Anzeige
HiSense dishwasher with plain-text display
SE 70 A 591
Design: W. Kaczmarek

Einbau-Backofen mit Sensorbedienung
Built-in oven with sensor operation
HB 66555
Design: F. Rieser, Gerd E. Wilsdorf

Sophisticated technology and extremely sensitive sensors take over lots of functions on Siemens appliances and thus play a decisive role in increased comfort. Functionality with impressive eye-appeal, such as the sensor system which functions without any knobs and switches. Or the dialogue display on the serie IQ washing machine, where you simply select the required programme on the menu, and the fully automatic programme selection in plain-text display integrated in the top edge of the door on the HiSense dishwasher. Details which help to shape the unmistakable character of Siemens appliances.

Standherd mit Gaskochzonen und Elektro-Backofen
Freestanding cooker with gas cooking zones and electric oven
HM 19550
Design: F. Rieser

Haushalt, Küche und Bad/Household, Kitchen and Bath

Siemens-Electrogeräte

Viessmann Werke

Anschrift/*Address*
D-35108 Allendorf (Eder)
Ansprechpartner/*Contact*
Helmut Weber
Telefon/*Phone*
+49 (0)6452/70 22 98
Telefax/*Fax*
+49 (0)6452/70 52 98
E-mail/*E-mail*
wee@viessmann.com
Internet/*Website*
www.viessmann.de
Gründungsdatum/*Foundation*
1917
Filiale/*Branch Office*
10 Werke im In- und Ausland, Vertriebsorganisationen in Deutschland und 33 weiteren Ländern, insgesamt 106 Niederlassungen
10 plants at home and abroad, marketing organization in Germany and 33 other countries, altogether 106 sales offices
Umsatz/*Turnover*
Über 1 Mrd. €
Over 1 billion €
Mitarbeiter/*Employees*
rund 6.800
around 6.800
Kunden/*Clients*
Eingetragene Heizungsfachfirmen
Registered heating experts
Tätigkeitsfelder/*Fields of Activity*
Heizkessel für Öl und Gas von 4 bis 15.000 kW sowie darauf abgestimmte Systemtechnik wie Brenner, Regelungen und Speicher-Wasserwärmer bis hin zu Solar-/ Lüftungssystemen, Wärmepumpen, Nah- und Fernwärme-Übergabestationen und Blockheizkraftwerken
Boilers for oil and gas from 4 to 15,000 kw as well as matching system technology such as burners, controls and storage warm water heaters up to solar ventilation systems, heat pumps, local and remote heat transfer stations and block heating plants.

Die Viessmann Gruppe ist mit rund 6800 Mitarbeitern weltweit einer der bedeutendsten Hersteller von Produkten der Heiztechnik. Der Name Viessmann steht weltweit für Kompetenz und Innovation. So bietet die Viessmann Gruppe ein komplettes Programm technologischer Spitzenprodukte und die exakt darauf abgestimmte Systemtechnik. Doch bei aller Vielfalt haben unsere Produkte eines gemeinsam: den durchgängig hohen Qualitätsstandard, der sich in Betriebssicherheit, Energieeinsparung, Umweltschonung und Bedienkomfort ausdrückt.

Das Vitotec-Programm ist die gelungene Synthese bewährter Spitzentechnik und zukunftsweisender Innovationen. Vitotec bildet die Einheit von Technik, Funktion und Design. Dabei ist der hohe Gebrauchsnutzen – gleichermaßen für den Heizungsfachmann wie für den Anlagenbetreiber – stets in den Vordergrund gestellt. So vereint sich in Vitotec funktionales Design und innovative Technik. Das Vitotec Design ist auf das Wesentliche reduziert und in einfachen geometrischen Grundformen gestaltet. Die Farbe „Vitosilber" signalisiert höchste Qualität und technischen Standard. „Vitorange" als Akzentfarbe greift Wärme und Tradition auf und ist weiteres Gestaltungselement für Wiedererkennung, Unverwechselbarkeit und Systemfähigkeit aller Vitotec-Produkte.

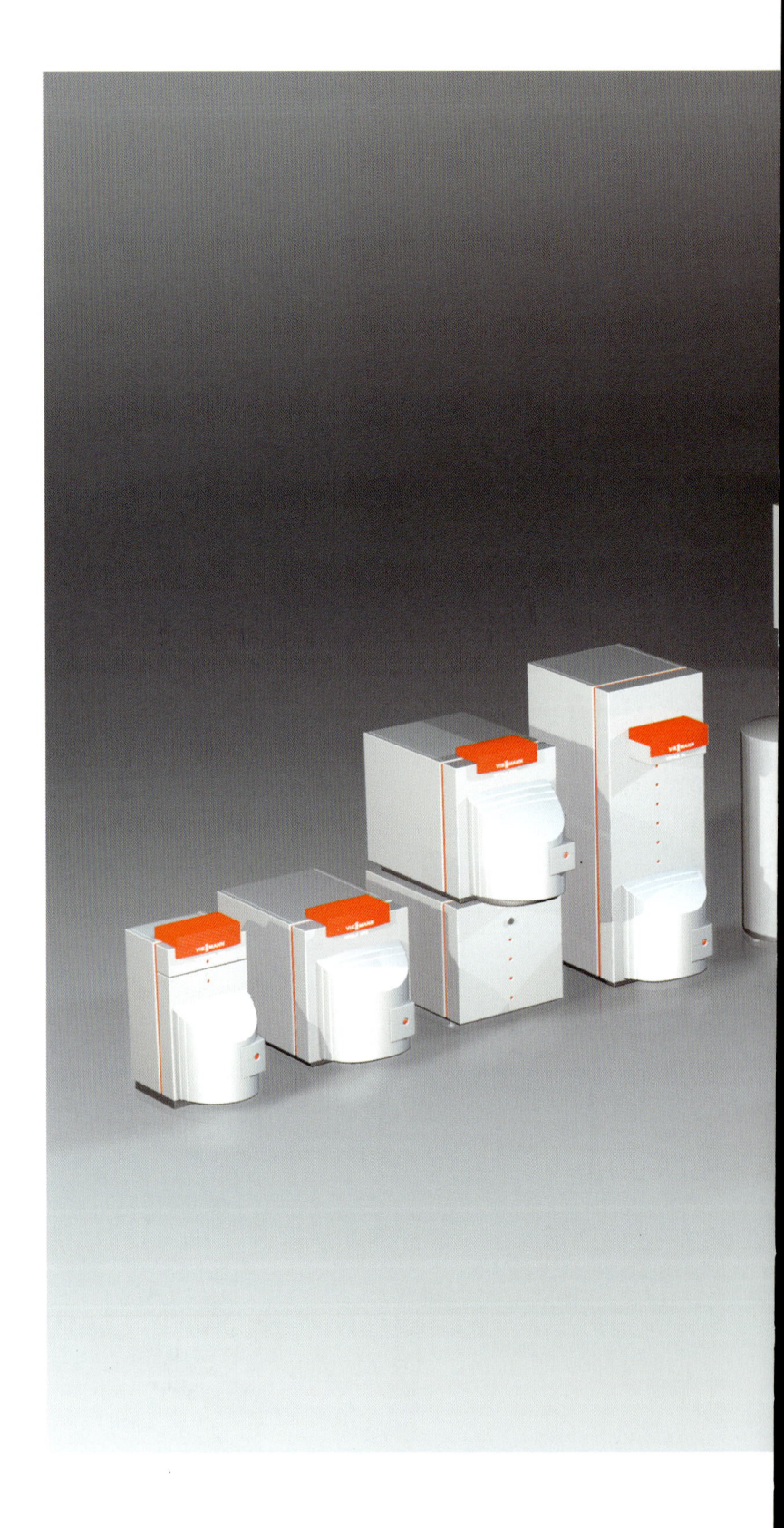

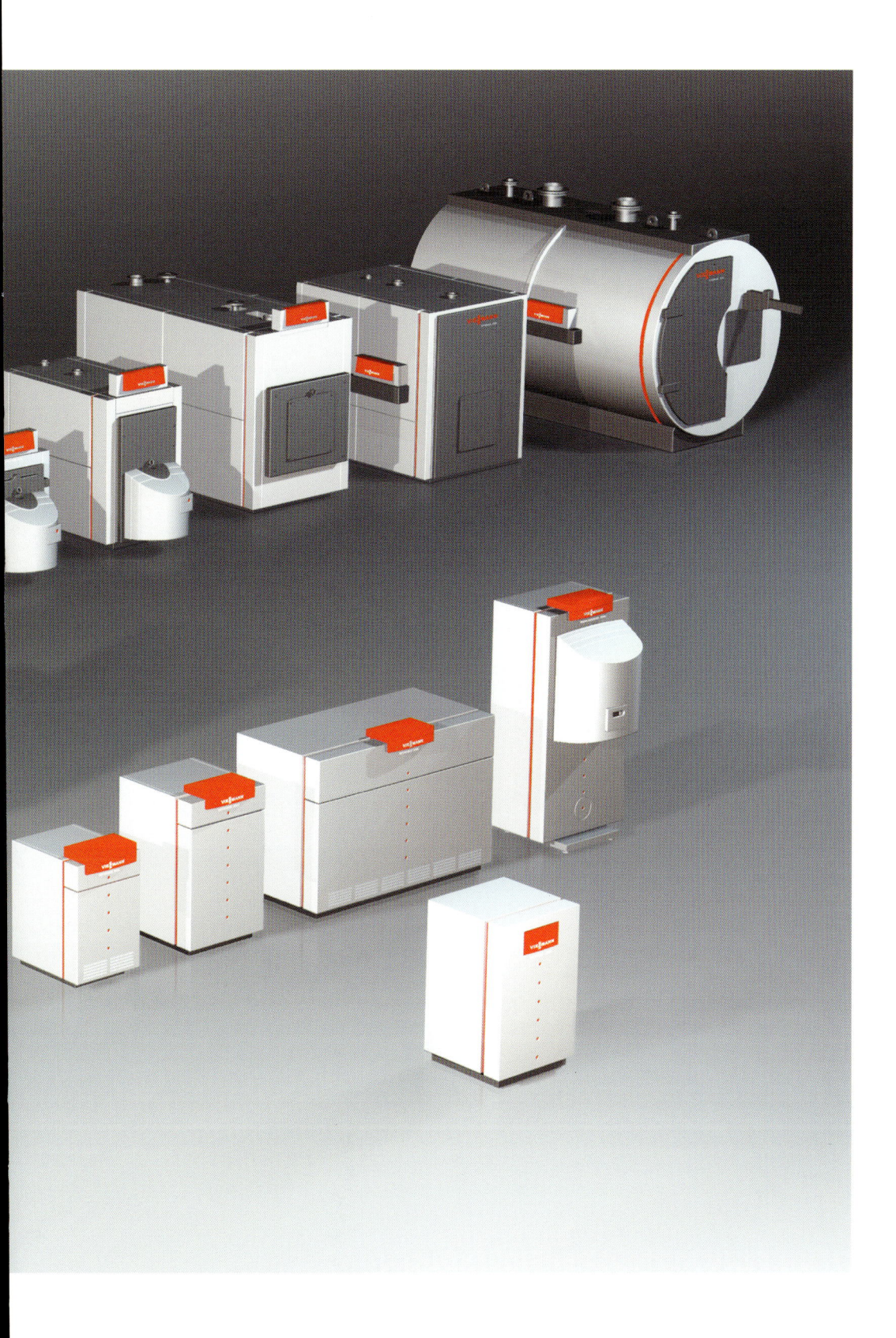

The Viessmann Group employs around 6800 staff and is one of the world's foremost manufacturers of heating equipment. The name Viessmann stands for expertise an innovation worldwide.
The Viessmann Group offers a complete range of top-quality, high-tech products along with perfectly matched modular system components. For all their diversity, our products have one thing in common - the consistently high quality which is expressed in operational reliability, energy savings, environmental compatibility and user-friendliness.

The Vitotec product range is the successful synthesis of proven high-tech engineering and future-oriented innovation. Vitotec is technology, function and design in perfect harmony, aimed constantly at providing significant benefits for both the heating engineer and the user. Vitotec combines functional design and innovative technology. The Vitotec design is reduced to the essential and contained within simple basic geometrical shapes. The "Vitosilver" colour finish reflects quality and progressive technology of the highest standard. The keynote colour "Vitorange" symbolizes warmth and tradition. It is another design element that underlines the recognition, uniqueness and system compatibility of all Vitotec products.

imperial-Werke oHG

Anschrift/*Address*
Borries-/Installstraße 10-18
D-32257 Bünde (Westfalen)

Ansprechpartner/*Contact*
Ole vom Baur

Telefon/*Phone*
+49 (0)5223/481-236

Telefax/*Fax*
+49 (0)5223/481-336

E-mail/*E-mail*
direct@imperial.de

Internet/*Website*
www.imperial.de

Tätigkeitsfelder/*Fields of Activity*
Küchen-Einbaugeräte
Built-in kitchen appliance

Hohe Ansprüche an Qualität und Funktionalität sind die Voraussetzungen für die Auswahl eines hochwertigen Einbaugerätes. Den Ausschlag gibt jedoch erfahrungsgemäß die Gestaltung des Produkts. Zukunftsweisendes Design zeichnet sich auch heute noch durch den einstigen Bauhaus-Leitsatz „Form folgt Funktion" aus. Gerade im anspruchsvolleren Segment zählt dabei nicht "Auffallen um jeden Preis", sondern eine Optik, die Trends setzt.

Das Unternehmen mit Hauptsitz im westfälischen Bünde produziert und vertreibt designstarke und hochwertige Einbaugeräte. Qualität, Funktionalität und Langlebigkeit sind dabei geradezu selbstverständlich. Den Nachweis führen die aktuellen ausgezeichneten Neuheiten.

CNT 5394 SVT, Autark-Touchtronic-Kochfeld
Autark-Touchtronic-Kochfeld mit Edelstahl-Rahmen. Es verfügt über vier runde Kochzonen mit HiLight-Beheizung für kurze Ankochzeiten und bessere Energie-Ausnutzung, u. a. mit 3-Kreis-Kochzone und rechteckiger Multi-Zone. Foto: imperial

CNT 5394 SVT, Touchtronic-Ceramic Hob
Touchtronic ceramic hob with stainless steel rim. Four circular cooking zones with HiLight elements for rapid heat up and more efficient use of energy. Also available with three circular zones and a rectangular multi-zone. Photo: imperial

DIY 966, Design-Insel-Dunstabzugshaube
Pure Eleganz von imperial: die Dunstabzugshaube im Pur-Design als Inselmodell. Im Bild in Edelstahl, im Programm auch in Aluminium mit Graphit-Glass. Nicht nur schön, sondern auch leistungsstark. Für ambitionierte Hobbyköche besonders schön zu Elementen aus dem MultiModul-System. Foto: imperial

DIY 966, Designer Island Cooker Hood
Pure elegance from imperial: the Pur-Design island cooker hood. Shown here in stainless steel, also available in aluminium with graphite glass. Both beautiful and powerful. Ideal for the keen cook, especially when combined with elements from the combiset range. Photo: imperial

B 8694-3 UT, Backofen

Für besondere Ansprüche: der Backofen Valido-Design in 90er Breite. Backbleche und Roste verschwinden in einem seitlichen Fach, das schwarze Glas lässt keine Einblicke zu. Nobel: die Kombination mit Edelstahl. Im Bild mit dem imperial-Multi-Bräter. Foto: imperial

B 8694-3 UT, Oven

A highly individual oven: the 90 cm wide Valido-Design oven. Baking trays and oven racks can be stored in the compartment at the side, hidden by the black glass. A stunning combination with stainless steel. Shown here with the imperial gourmet oven dish. Photo: imperial

When it comes to choosing a top of the range built in appliance, one naturally expects the best in terms of quality and function. But in our experience it is the finish of the product that is the deciding factor. Innovative design today still stands out for its adherence to the old Bauhaus philosophy of „Form follows function". The top end of the market in particular is not interested in making an impact at any price, but rather in creating a look that will set a trend.

The company, based in the Westphalian town of Bünde, produces appliances that are distinguished by their high value and excellent design. Quality, functionality and longevity are taken for granted. And the design accolades awarded to our new products are proof of this philosophy.

BDGL 8664-2 UT, Backofen-Dampf-Druckgarer-Kombination

Zwei Geräte in einem: das Kombinationsgerät im Valido-Design. Optisch eine Einheit, verbirgt sich hinter der oberen Lifttür der Dampf-Druckgarer. Das Innere des darunter eingebauten Backofens wird durch das dunkle Glas erst bei Betrieb sichtbar. Foto: imperial

BDGL 8664-2 UT, Oven-Steam Oven Combination

Two appliances in one: the Valido-Design oven-steam oven combination. Has the appearance of a single appliance, but hiding behind the lift-up door at the top is the steam oven. The interior of the built in oven below is concealed by the dark glass when not in use. Photo: imperial

Robert Bosch Hausgeräte GmbH

Anschrift/*Address*
Hochstraße 17
D-81669 München

Ansprechpartner/*Contact*
Presse: Uta Rodenhäuser

Telefon/*Phone*
+49 (0)89/45 90-28 08

Ansprechpartner/*Contact*
Design: Roland Vetter

Telefon/*Phone*
+49 (0)7322/92-25 52

Telefax/*Fax*
+49 (0)89/45 90-29 57

E-mail/*E-mail*
bosch-pr@bshg.com

Internet/*Website*
www.bosch-hausgeraete.de

Sympathische Grundwerte in Verbindung mit überragender Technik – so versteht sich die moderne Marke BOSCH in ihrer Tradition.

Die hohe, verlässliche Qualität der Geräte besteht auf ständig verbesserten Materialien und Oberflächen, herausragenden Ingenieurleistungen und langjährige vielfältige Erfahrungen.

Die sich selbsterklärenden, logisch und verständlich gestalteten Bedieneinheiten bieten höchsten Kundennutzen und bewirken zugleich eine Faszination und Akzeptanz modernster Technik.

Schonung der natürlichen Ressourcen, nicht nur im Herstellungsprozess der Geräte, sondern speziell im alltäglichen Gebrauch sind oberstes Gebot der Marke BOSCH.

Die zeitgemäße, moderne Formensprache, perfekt modulierte Greifformen, kontrastreiche Anzeigeelemente, präzise stabile Formverbindungen und größtmögliche Servicefreundlichkeit prägen den unverwechselbaren Charakter der BOSCH-Hausgeräte.

KSW 38920 Wein-Lagerschrank/*Wine cooler*

SGS 56A25 Stand-Geschirrspüler/*Dishwasher*

Appealing fundamental values in conjunction with outstanding technology - this is how the modern brand, BOSCH regards itself in terms of its tradition.

The high, reliable quality of the appliances is based on continuously improved materials and surface finishes, outstanding engineering and many years of varied experience.

The self-explanatory, logical and comprehensively designed operating controls offer maximum user-friendliness and simultaneously, inspire a fascination for and acceptance of advanced technology.

Husbanding natural resources, not only in the product manufacturing process but in daily use, especially, is the central precept of the BOSCH brand.

The contemporary modern design language, perfectly fashioned handle styles, richly contrasted display elements, precise, stable style combinations and the greatest possible service-friendliness mark the distinctive character of BOSCH domestic appliances.

Haushalt, Küche und Bad/*Household, Kitchen and Bath*

Robert Bosch Hausgeräte

WMF Württembergische Metallwarenfabrik AG

Anschrift/*Address*
Eberhardstraße
D-73309 Geislingen/Steige

Ansprechpartner/*Contact*
Peter Tatzelt
Tina Schütz

Telefon/*Phone*
+49 (0)7331/25-87 10
+49 (0)7331/25-88 16

Telefax/*Fax*
+49 (0)7331/25-89 97

E-mail/*E-mail*
p.tatzelt@wmf.de
t.schuetz@wmf.de

Internet/*Website*
www.wmf.de

Gründungsdatum/*Foundation*
1853 durch Straub & Sohn, Geislingen
1853 from Straub & Sohn, Geislingen

Mitarbeiter/*Employees*
5.094, 4.448 im Inland
(Stand: 30.11.2002)
5,094, 4,448 inland
(status quo: 30.11.2002)

Filiale/*Branch Office*
146 in Deutschland
146 in Germany

Umsatz/*Turnover*
571,5 Mio. € (in 2001)
34,2 % Auslandsgeschäft
571.5 million € (in 2001)
34.2 % foreign business

Tätigkeitsfelder/*Fields of Activity*
Konsum- und Objektgeschäft
Consumer and object business

WMF liefert ein umfangreiches Sortiment mit Schwerpunkt Tisch und Küche für den privaten und gewerblichen Bereich. Der Vertrieb erfolgt über eigene Verkaufsfilialen, über den Facheinzelhandel, Warenhäuser und ausgewählte Versender. Im Ausland verfügt WMF über Vertriebsgesellschaften in Europa und den USA. Im Gastronomie- und Hotelbereich gehört WMF weltweit zu den führenden Ausstattern der Gastronomie und internationalen Hotelketten.

In diesem Jahr kann das Unternehmen auf eine 150-jährige erfolgreiche Entwicklung zurückblicken. Seit der Gründung 1853 versteht sich WMF als ein Anbieter von Produkten, die sich in Design, Qualität und Gebrauchsnutzen vom Wettbewerb differenzieren. Die WMF-Produktentwicklung mit hauseigenem Atelier arbeitet schon seit den zwanziger Jahren mit renommierten Designern im In- und Ausland zusammen. Dem Ruf der Qualität, Zuverlässigkeit, Fortschrittlichkeit und Innovation fühlt sich WMF wie in den vergangenen 150 Jahren auch in Zukunft weiterhin verpflichtet.

Butter- und Zuckerdose aus der Frühstücksserie Kult von WMF
Ein kultiviertes Frühstück ist ein gelungener Start in den Tag. Die richtigen Gerätschaften dazu, wie die Butter- und Zuckerdose, bietet WMF mit Kult, den Accessoires für Frühstück und Brunch. Richtig cool die klare und dennoch weiche Formgebung der Gerätschaften aus mattem Edelstahl in Verbindung mit brillantem Bleikristall.
Material: Cromargan® Edelstahl und Bleikristall
Design: Sebastian Bergne, London

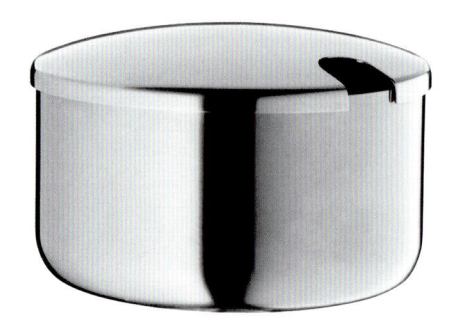

Butter dish and sugar bowl of the breakfast range Kult by WMF
A stylish breakfast is a good start for a new day.
WMF Kult gives you the appropriate accessories for breakfast and brunch. The clear, yet soft shapes of the articles, made of matt stainless steel in combination with brilliant crystal, that's really cool.
Material: Cromargan® 18/10 stainless steel and brilliant crystal.
Design: Sebastian Bergne, London

Ceramill® von WMF im coolen Design

Die Ceramill®-Erfolgsgeschichte wird fortgesetzt: Die neuen Ceramill®-Mühlen präsentieren sich in modernem, coolem Design. Das Mahlwerk befindet sich im oberen Teil der Mühle, sodass beim Nachwürzen keine lästigen Krümel auf den Tisch kommen. Befüllt wird die Mühle ebenfalls von oben.
Die neuen Ceramill®-Mühlen sind mit dem bewährten Crush Grind-Mahlwerk ausgestattet, auf das die WMF 10 Jahre Garantie gibt.
Material: Cromargan®/ Glas
Design: Metz und Kindler, Darmstadt

Ceramill® from WMF in a Cool Design

The Ceramill® success story continues: the new Ceramill® spice mills appear in a design that is modern and cool. The grinding mechanism is in the top of the mill so it stops tiresome crumbs from being scattered over the table when seasoning.
The mills can be filled at the top, too.
The new Ceramill® mills are also equipped with the tried and tested Crush Grind Mechanism that WMF guarantees for 10 years.
Material: Cromargan® 18/10 stainless steel and glass
Design: Metz und Kindler, Darmstadt

Concept:
ein Topf für jeden Herd

Concept, die neue Kochgeschirrserie von WMF ist ein wahrer Alleskönner. Ausgestattet mit dem neuartigen TransTherm® Allherdboden ist Concept für alle Herdarten gleichermaßen geeignet: Für Gas, Ceran, Elektro und Induktion. Auffallendes Designmerkmal dieser geradlinigen Kochgeschirrserie ist der große Deckelgriff, der gleichzeitig für optimale Handhabung sorgt. Ebenfalls ein Novum bei WMF-Töpfen: Concept ist die erste Kochgeschirr-Serie mit integriertem, versenktem Steckdeckel im Topfkörper.
Design: Metz und Kindler Produktdesign, Darmstadt

Concept: a pot for every occasion

Concept, the new pot range by WMF, is a real contortionist. Equipped with the new TransTherm® all-stove bottom, Concept is suitable for all stove types: for gas, glasstop (Ceran), electric and induction-type.
A distinguishing design feature is the handle on the lid, which additionally provides good ergonomic qualities.
Also a novelty amongst WMF pots: Concept is the first pot range with integrated, flush-fitting lids.
Design: Metz und Kindler Produktdesign, Darmstadt

WMF manufactures an extensive range of products, with the main emphasis on kitchen and tableware items for both private and commercial use. The products are sold through company-owned retail outlets, specialist retailers, department stores and selected mail order companies. Abroad, WMF has subsidiaries in Europe and the USA. In the hotel and restaurant sector, WMF is one of the worlds leading suppliers to restaurants and international hotel chains.

This year the company can view back on its 150-year success-story. Since it was founded in 1853, WMF has forged its reputation as a manufacturer of products, the design, quality and utility of which set the company apart from its competitors. From as far back as the 1920s to the present day, WMF's product development department has collaborated with renowned designers at home and abroad at its own design studios. WMF continues to remain committed to the principles of quality, reliability, progress and innovation. This is a 150-year old committing tradition, which means distinction for the past and the future.

Haushalt, Küche und Bad/ Household, Kitchen and Bath

WMF Württembergische Metallwarenfabrik AG

Anschrift/*Address*
Eberhardstraße
D-73309 Geislingen/Steige

Ansprechpartner/*Contact*
Peter Tatzelt
Tina Schütz

Telefon/*Phone*
+49 (0)7331/25-87 10
+49 (0)7331/25-88 16

Telefax/*Fax*
+49 (0)7331/25-89 97

E-mail/*E-mail*
p.tatzelt@wmf.de
t.schuetz@wmf.de

Internet/*Website*
www.wmf.de

Gründungsdatum/*Foundation*
1853 durch Straub & Sohn, Geislingen
1853 from Straub & Sohn, Geislingen

Mitarbeiter/*Employees*
5.094, 4.448 im Inland
(Stand: 30.11.2002)
*5,094, 4,448 inland
(status quo: 30.11.2002)*

Filiale/*Branch Office*
146 in Deutschland
146 in Germany

Umsatz/*Turnover*
571,5 Mio. € (in 2001)
34,2 % Auslandsgeschäft
*571.5 million € (in 2001)
34.2 % foreign business*

Tätigkeitsfelder/*Fields of Activity*
Konsum- und Objektgeschäft
Consumer and object business

WMF liefert ein umfangreiches Sortiment mit Schwerpunkt Tisch und Küche für den privaten und gewerblichen Bereich. Der Vertrieb erfolgt über eigene Verkaufsfilialen, über den Facheinzelhandel, Warenhäuser und ausgewählte Versender. Im Ausland verfügt WMF über Vertriebsgesellschaften in Europa und den USA.
Im Gastronomie- und Hotelbereich gehört WMF weltweit zu den führenden Ausstattern der Gastronomie und internationalen Hotelketten.

In diesem Jahr kann das Unternehmen auf eine 150-jährige erfolgreiche Entwicklung zurückblicken. Seit der Gründung 1853 versteht sich WMF als ein Anbieter von Produkten, die sich in Design, Qualität und Gebrauchsnutzen vom Wettbewerb differenzieren. Die WMF-Produktentwicklung mit hauseigenem Atelier arbeitet schon seit den zwanziger Jahren mit renommierten Designern im In- und Ausland zusammen. Dem Ruf der Qualität, Zuverlässigkeit, Fortschrittlichkeit und Innovation fühlt sich WMF wie in den vergangenen 150 Jahren auch in Zukunft weiterhin verpflichtet.

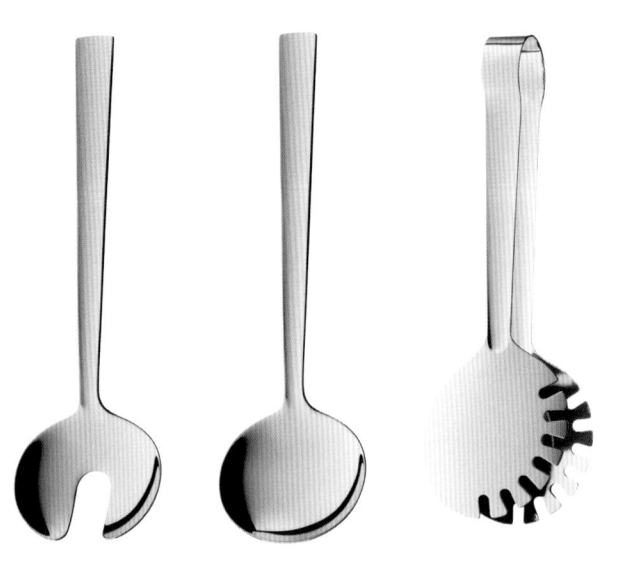

Aus Lust am Kombinieren - combiNation von WMF
Das Besteck-Konzept combiNation von WMF ist das Besteck der 1000 Möglichkeiten. Es bietet viele verschiedene Teile für die ganz individuellen Gewohnheiten an.
Bei combiNation werden die Teile nach Geschmack und Gewohnheit ausgewählt - so viel man will.
Alle 54 verschiedenen Teile sind miteinander kombinierbar, passen also zueinander. Selbst für nicht alltägliche Spezialitäten gibt es geeignete Besteckteile zum Essen und Servieren.
Für das klare, sachliche und funktionale Design von combiNation zeichnet der Däne Ole Palsby verantwortlich. Die leichte Wölbung und die abgerundeten Kanten machen das Besteck weich und lassen es angenehm in der Hand liegen. Das vollendete Zusammenspiel von Ästhetik und Funktionalität macht die besondere Qualität von combiNation aus. combiNation ist die neue Dimension eines altbekannten Gebrauchsgegenstandes - die Vision einer Zukunft, die schon angebrochen ist.
Material: Cromargan®
Design: Ole Palsby, Dänemark

*The fun is in the combining -
combiNation by WMF
combiNation by WMF, the innovative concept of cutlery, puts a stop to compromise. combiNation is the cutlery with 1000 possibilities. It offers a range of different pieces for quite individual needs.
With combiNation you select the pieces according to taste and habit - as many as you wish. All 54 pieces can be combined with each other - so they all match.
Even for specialties that are a bit out of the ordinary there are the right pieces of cutlery for eating and serving.
The simple, practical and functional design of combiNation is the work of the Dane Ole Palsby. The light curved shape and the rounded edges give the cutlery a softness and a comfortable feeling when held. The complete interaction of aesthetics and functionally are characteristic of the special quality of combiNation.
combiNation is the new dimension of the old familiar article - the vision of the future which has already begun.
Material: Cromargan®
Design: Ole Palsby, Denmark*

**Aus dem Kühlschrank auf den Tisch:
Frischhalten und Servieren mit Top Serve von WMF**

Vielseitig, praktisch und gleichzeitig chic: das Frischhalte- und Serviersystem Top Serve von WMF wird vielerlei Anforderungen gerecht. Wurst, Käse, Vorspeisen, Salate, Desserts und noch viel mehr können darin im Kühlschrank praktisch aufbewahrt und lange frisch gehalten werden.
In den Glasschalen mit Frischhaltedeckel ist der Inhalt dabei gut sichtbar. Man hat jederzeit einen guten Überblick über die Vorräte.
Vorbereitete Speisen werden direkt aus dem Kühlschrank bei Tisch serviert. Reste vom Vortag werden in der Schale - ohne Deckel - einfach in die Mikrowelle gestellt und warm auf den Tisch gebracht. Für den Backofen sind die Schalen nicht geeignet.
Das neuartige Frischhalte-Ventil im Deckel stellt einen leichten Unterdruck her. Somit ist der Inhalt luftdicht verschlossen und bleibt lange appetitlich frisch. Zum Verschließen wird der Deckel aufgesetzt und das Frische-Ventil nach unten gedrückt. Beim Öffnen zieht man das Ventil nach oben.
Die Schalen aus Glas sind absolut geruchs- und geschmacksneutral, beständig gegen Farbstoffe und nehmen es auch nicht übel, wenn mit Messer und Gabel darin hantiert wird. Sie verlieren deshalb auch nach längerem Gebrauch nichts von ihrer attraktiven Optik.
Der Deckel aus Cromargan® Edelstahl Rostfrei 18/10 ist unverwüstlich, pflegeleicht und hygienisch.
Die Schalen gibt es in folgenden Größen: rund mit 13, 15 und 18 cm Ø und eckig in den Maßen 13x10, 21x13 und 26x21 cm.
Die runden Schalen sind auch als 2teiliges Set (Ø 15 und 18 cm) erhältlich.
Material: Cromargan®/ Glas.
Design: Achim Bölstler, Werksdesign

From the ridge to the table: Storing and serving with WMF Top Serve
Versatile, practical and at the same time stylish: the WMF Top Serve storage and serving system can be put to use in a variety of ways. You can use it to store sausage (cold meats), cheese, starters, salads, deserts and a whole lot more and to keep them fresh in the fridge for much longer. The contents are clearly visible in the glass bowls with the "keep fresh" lids so you are fully aware all of the time what you have left.
Prepared food can go straight from the fridge onto the table. Place your leftovers from the previous day in a bowl and place it in the microwave - without the lid - to serve them warm. The bowls are not suitable for oven use.
The innovate "keep fresh" valve in the lid produces a slight vacuum and the contents stay absolutely fresh and airtight much longer. To close, put the lid on and press the "keep fresh" valve. To open, pull the valve upwards.
The glass bowls are completely non-toxic, resistant to food coloring and are scratch resistant if you use a knife and fork in them. Even after prolonged use they still look attractive.
The Cromargan® 18/10 stainless steel lid is durable, easy to clean and hygienic. The bowls are available in the following sizes: round with diameters of 13, 15 and 18 cm, and rectangular measuring 13x10, 21x13 and 26x21 cm. The round bowls are also available as a set of two (15 and 18 cm in diameter).
Material: Cromargan® 18/10 stainless steel and glass
Design: Achim Bölstler, Werksdesign

WMF manufactures an extensive range of products, with the main emphasis on kitchen and tableware items for both private and commercial use. The products are sold through company-owned retail outlets, specialist retailers, department stores and selected mail order companies. Abroad, WMF has subsidiaries in Europe and the USA. In the hotel and restaurant sector, WMF is one of the worlds leading suppliers to restaurants and international hotel chains.

This year the company can view back on its 150-year success-story. Since it was founded in 1853, WMF has forged its reputation as a manufacturer of products, the design, quality and utility of which set the company apart from its competitors. From as far back as the 1920s to the present day, WMF's product development department has collaborated with renowned designers at home and abroad at its own design studios. WMF continues to remain committed to the principles of quality, reliability, progress and innovation. This is a 150-year old committing tradition, which means distinction for the past and the future.

Hoesch Metall+Kunststoffwerk GmbH & Co.

Anschrift/*Address*
Postfach 10 04 24
D-52304 Düren

Ansprechpartner/*Contact*
Stephan Herwartz

Telefon/*Phone*
+49 (0)2422/54-311

Telefax/*Fax*
+49 (0)2422/54-319

E-mail/*E-mail*
stephan.herwartz@hoesch.de

Internet/*Website*
www.hoesch.de

Ein Bad nehmen, träumen, genießen: kaum etwas trägt mehr zur Erholung bei. Gleichzeitig ist nichts so individuell wie Entspannung in den eigenen vier Wänden – ob in Badewanne, Whirlpool oder Römischem Dampfbad.

International anerkannte Designer liefern Hoesch ihre Ideen, exzellente Werkstoffe sind das Medium, mit dem sie zur Realität werden. Und handwerkliche Perfektion lässt die Qualität entstehen, die unsere Partner und Kunden von uns erwarten.

Bathroom Foster

Das Bad von Norman Foster, einem der großen Designer unserer Zeit. Klare Eleganz durch einfache geometrische Formen.

Individualität in der Badewanne von Foster. Mit Wandanschluss oder im klassischen Oval. Freistehend oder mit Außen-Verkleidung. Großzügig ausgeformt und bequem im Einstieg. Die intelligente Wannenrandgestaltung bietet Raum für Armaturen oder Accessoires. Aus hochwertigem Sanitäracryl.

Die durchgängige Formensprache des Ovals, entwickelt aus zwei nebeneinanderliegenden Kreisen, auch beim Dampfbad. Filigran und leicht in der Wirkung. Mit besonders flacher Dampfdüse und Seitenbrausen, die elegant in die Profile integriert sind.

The bathroom by Norman Foster, one of the great designers of our time. Clear elegance through simple geometric form.
The individuality of bathtubs by Foster. Wall-mounted or in a classic oval. Free-standing with surround, or as a fitted version. Generously proportioned and easy to get into. The intelligent bath rim design allows space for fittings or accessories. Made from a high-quality sanitary acrylic.
The universal language of the oval, developed from two adjoining circles, is also suitable for steam baths. Delicate and with an essence of lightness. With a particularly flat steam nozzle and side jets elegantly integrated into the contour.

Aviva

Aviva steht für Lebenskunst und Freude. Die runde Üppigkeit der Badewanne wird ergänzt durch Lehnen, die den Kopf- und Nackenbereich unterstützen. Das unvergleichliche Badevergnügen gibt es auch als Vorwand- und Eckvariante und natürlich auch mit Whirlsystem.

Aviva stands for joy and the art of living. The generous size of the round bathtub is complemented by supports for the head and neck area. This incomparable bathing experience is available in free-standing and corner variations and naturally with the whirl system.

Enjoying a nice bath and daydreaming: nothing else is better for relaxation. And nothing is better than relaxing within your own four walls – whether it's in a bathtub, a whirlpool or a Roman steam bath.

Internationally recognized designers deliver Hoesch the ideas, excellent raw materials are the medium that turns them into reality. And perfect craftsmanship produces the quality that our partners and customers expect from us.

Modula

Außen klare Linien, innen unglaublich vielfältig. Das ist Modula. Vorbildliche Ergonomie und anspruchsvolle Ästhetik, dazu ein komplettes Accessoire-Programm, das teilweise nachgerüstet werden kann. Aus Sanitäracryl – farbecht, stabil und sehr pflegeleicht. Für jeden Lebensumstand und für jedes Alter.

Clear lines outside, unbelievably variable inside. This is Modula. Superb ergonomics and sophisticated aesthetics complemented by a complete modular accessories system that can be added to or changed at will. Made from a high-quality sanitary acrylic, colorfast, enduring and very easy to care for. For people of any age and circumstance.

Haushalt, Küche und Bad / Household, Kitchen and Bath

Hoesch Metall + Kunststoffwerk

Miele

Haushalt, Küche und Bad / Household, Kitchen and Bathroom

Miele & Cie.

Anschrift/*Address*
Carl-Miele-Straße 29
D-33332 Gütersloh

Ansprechpartner/*Contact*
Frido Jacobs

Telefon/*Phone*
+49 (0)5241/89-41 41

Telefax/*Fax*
+49 (0)5241/89-41 40

E-mail/*E-mail*
info@miele.de

Internet/*Website*
www.miele.de

Gründungsdatum/*Foundation*
1899

Umsatz/*Turnover*
2,24 Milliarden Euro
(Geschäftsjahr 2001/2002)

Mitarbeiterzahl/*Employees*
15.328

Kunden/*Clients*
Fachhandel
Specialist dealers

Filialen/*Branch Offices*
14 Vertriebszentren
in Deutschland
31 ausländische
Vertriebsniederlassungen
14 Area Sales Offices in Germany
31 Foreign Subsidiaries

"Klasse statt Masse", oder anders ausgedrückt Qualität statt Quantität, bestimmt die Erfolgsformel des Unternehmens Miele & Cie. seit der Gründung 1899. Mit diesem Unternehmensgrundsatz hat sich das Familienunternehmen Miele den Weg zu einem der führenden europäischen Hausgeräteherstelle bereitet - durch Konzentration auf ein Geräteangebot mit hohem Leistungsniveau und richtungsweisender Technologie. Durch das Streben hin zu Qualitätsprodukten mit fortschrittlicher Hausgerätetechnik und einem immer höheren Gebrauchsnutzen ist Miele zu einem Markenanbieter geworden, der sich aus der Masse des Marktangebotes hervorhebt: Modernste Technik, fortschrittliches Design und die sprichwörtliche Langlebigkeit der Produkte werden unterstrichen durch ein Höchstmaß an Funktionalität und Gebrauchsnutzen. Das Produktspektrum umfasst u.a. Waschmaschinen, Wäschetrockner, Geschirrspüler, Küchen-Einbau- und -Standgeräte zum Kochen und Kühlen, Staubsauger sowie gewerbliche Wäschepflege- und Spülgeräte.

Dunstabzugshaube DA 279
Cooker hood DA 279

Dunstabzugshaube DA 289
„Kopffreiheit"
Cooker hood DA 289
„Headroom"

Kochmulde KM 550
Hob unit KM 550

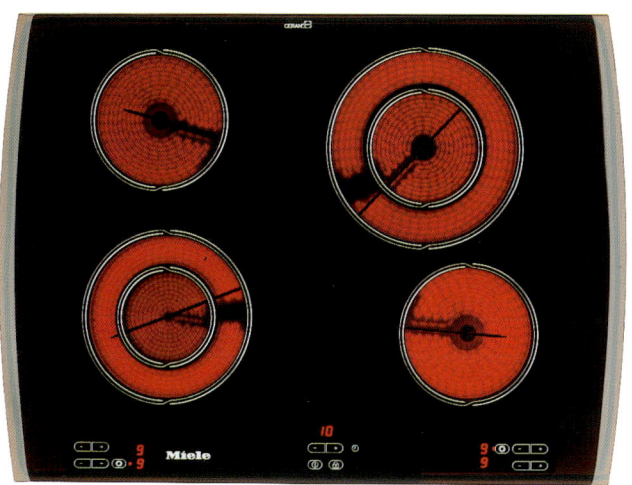

Kochmulde KM 548
Hob unit KM 548

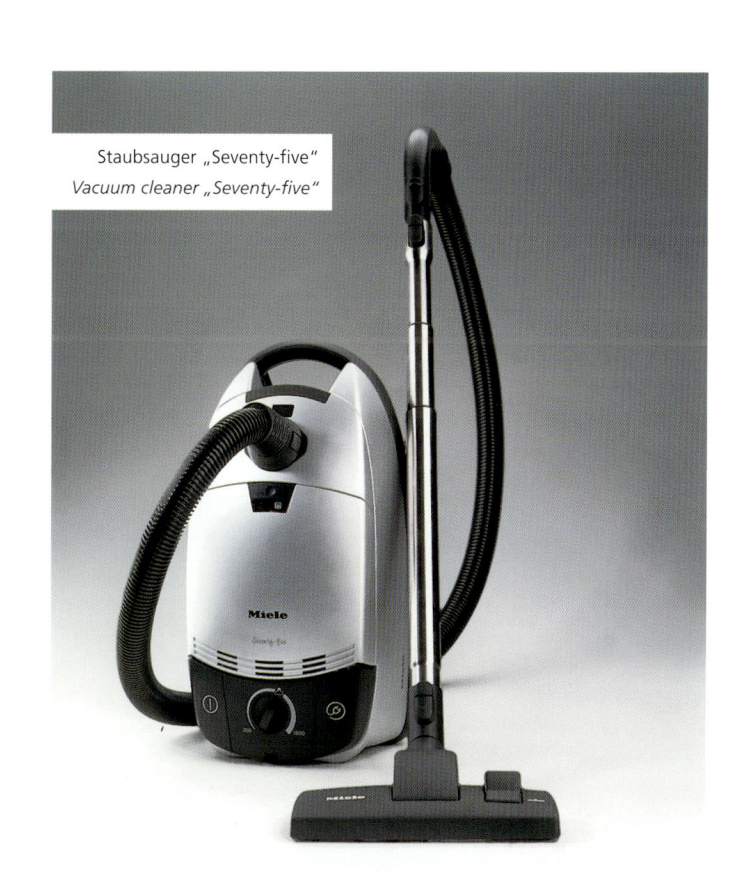

Staubsauger „Seventy-five"
Vacuum cleaner „Seventy-five"

The maxim "Quality rather than quantity" has been the formula for success at Miele & Cie. ever since the company was founded in 1899. This philosophy has paved the way for the family-run company Miele to become one of the leading white goods manufacturers in Europe, success achieved thanks to concentration on an appliance range offering the highest quality standards and future-proof technology. By endeavoring to produce quality products equipped with state-of-the-art household appliance technology and an increasing number of user benefits, Miele has become a supplier who stands head and shoulders above the mass of other brands on the market: state-of-the-art technology, progressive design and products renowned for their durability go hand in glove with a high degree of functionality and user convenience. The product range includes washing machines, tumble dryers, dishwashers, built-in and freestanding kitchen appliances for cooking and refrigeration, vacuum cleaners as well as commercial laundry-care machines and dishwashers.

Public Design
Public Design

Rang/*Rank*

Willy Meyer + Sohn / D-Hemer / 192 Punkte/*Points*	1
Wall / D-Berlin / 192 Punkte/*Points*	1
Hess Form + Licht / D-Villingen-Schwenningen / 188 Punkte/*Points*	3
MABEG Kreuschner / D-Soest / 180 Punkte/*Points*	4
Hawle Armaturen / D-Freilassing / 144 Punkte/*Points*	5
ufo unbegrenzt flexible Objekte / D-Langenhagen / 136 Punkte/*Points*	6
SPECTRAL GESELLSCHAFT FÜR LICHTTECHNIK / D-Freiburg / 128 Punkte/*Points*	7
Artemide / D-Fröndenberg / 124 Punkte/*Points*	8
Leitner / D-Waiblingen / 106 Punkte/*Points*	9

Hess Form + Licht GmbH

Anschrift/Address
Schlachthausstraße 19-19/3
D-78050 Villingen-Schwenningen

Ansprechpartner/Contact
Andreas Schmidt
Leitung Marketing/Marketing Director

Telefon/Phone
+49 (0)7721/920-0

Telefax/Fax
+49 (0)7721/920-250

E-mail/E-mail
hess@hess-form-licht.de

Internet/Website
www.hess-form-licht.de

Gründungsdatum/Foundation
1947

Filiale/Branch Office
Unternehmenssitz
in Villingen-Schwenningen
Produktion in Villingen-Schwenningen,
Löbau/Sachsen, Shelby/North Carolina
Eigene Niederlassungen in Frankreich,
Italien, Spanien und den USA
*Headquarters
in Villingen-Schwenningen
Production facilities in
Villingen-Schwenningen and Löbau/
Saxony, Germany, Shelby/North Carolina
Own branch offices in France, Italy,
Spain and the USA*

Umsatz/Turnover
2002: 39,0 Mio
2002: 39 million EUR

Mitarbeiter/Employees
2002: 220

Kunden/Clients
Architekten, Garten- und Landschafts-
architekten, Kommunen, Energiever-
sorgungsunternehmen, Ingenieur- und
Planungsbüros, Lichtplaner etc.
*Architects, landscape architects,
municipal governments, power utilities,
engineers and planning authorities,
lighting planners, etc.*

Ausstattung/Equipment
Modernes lichttechnisches Labor,
eigene Gießerei, 33 Außendienst-
mitarbeiter in Deutschland
*Modern research and development
facility for lighting technology, foundry,
33 sales representatives throughout
Germany*

Tätigkeitsfelder/Fields of Activity
Produktion und Vertrieb von Außen-/
Innenleuchten und Stadtmobiliar
*Manufacturing and sale of outdoor/
interior lighting fixtures and outdoor
furnishings*

Hess Form + Licht ist einer der international führenden Hersteller von gestalteten Außenleuchten. Mit einem breitgefächerten Leuchtenangebot erfüllt das Unternehmen alle Anforderungen an die Lichtgestaltung im öffentlichen Freiraum einschließlich der Objektbeleuchtung. Architekten, Planer und Bauherren verbinden die Marke Hess mit innovativer Lichttechnik und hochwertigem Design. Sie schätzen darüber hinaus die Funktionalität und Langlebigkeit der Produkte sowie die individuelle Projektunterstützung. Neben der konsequenten Weiterentwicklung der klassischen Straßen-, Wege- und Platzbeleuchtung setzt sich Hess intensiv mit Licht als Gestaltungselement auseinander. Auf der Basis modernster LED- und Scheinwerfer-Technologie ermöglicht das Unternehmen anspruchsvolle Lichtinszenierungen. Die Einbeziehung der Architektur spielt dabei eine zentrale Rolle. Es entsteht eine neue Erlebnisdimension, die öffentliche Räume bei Nacht in lebendige, unverwechselbare Schauplätze verwandelt. Einen wichtigen Beitrag zur Atmosphäre und Identität von Plätzen, Fußgängerzonen und Parks leistet Hess nicht zuletzt durch formal auf die Leuchten abgestimmtes Stadtmobiliar und Begrünungssysteme. Hess ist damit einer der wenigen Hersteller, die ganzheitliche Konzepte in der Stadt- und Freiraumgestaltung realisieren können.

Sedi Q, Collection Avangardo, Design Karsten Winkels
Wandeinbauleuchte mit prägnanter Gussoptik, außergewöhnlicher Lichtwirkung und robuster Konstruktion zur Ausleuchtung von Wegen, Gängen und Treppen (Ehrenpreis für Produktdesign 2001, Design Zentrum Nordrhein-Westfalen)
Recessed wall luminaires with precision cast appearance, extraordinary lighting effects and solid construction for the illumination of walkways, passages and stairs (awarded with Product Design prize by the Design Zentrum Nordrhein-Westfalen)

Baumscheibe und Absperrpoller Serpo,
Serpo tree grates and barrier bollards
Design Jean-Michel Wilmotte
Durchgängige Designlinie mit eleganter Form, unverwechselbarem Ornament und perfekter Funktion (red dot für hohe Designqualität 2002, Design Zentrum Nordrhein-Westfalen)
Consistent decorative design with elegant shapes, unmistakable ornamentation and practical function (red dot for Exceptional Design Quality in 2002, Design Zentrum Nordrhein-Westfalen)

Faro, Design Karsten Winkels
Systemleuchtenfamilie mit neuartigem lichttechnischem Konzept, das jegliche Blendung vermeidet und damit die Aufenthaltsqualität von Straßen und Plätzen bei Dunkelheit wesentlich verbessert
(iF DESIGN PLUS 2002, International Forum Design Hannover, red dot für hohe Designqualität 2002, Design Zentrum Nordrhein-Westfalen,
iF Design Award 2003, International Forum Design Hannover)
With this new family of outdoor luminaires, Hess, once again, displays its prowess in lighting.
The Faro features glare-free illumination made possible by the clever combination of secondary reflector and the splitting of the light spot image. In practice, this innovative product distinctly improves the atmosphere of streets and spaces at night
(iF DESIGN PLUS 2002, International Forum Design Hanover, red dot for Exceptional Design Quality 2002, Design Zentrum Nordrhein-Westfalen,
iF Design Award 2003, International Forum Design Hanover)

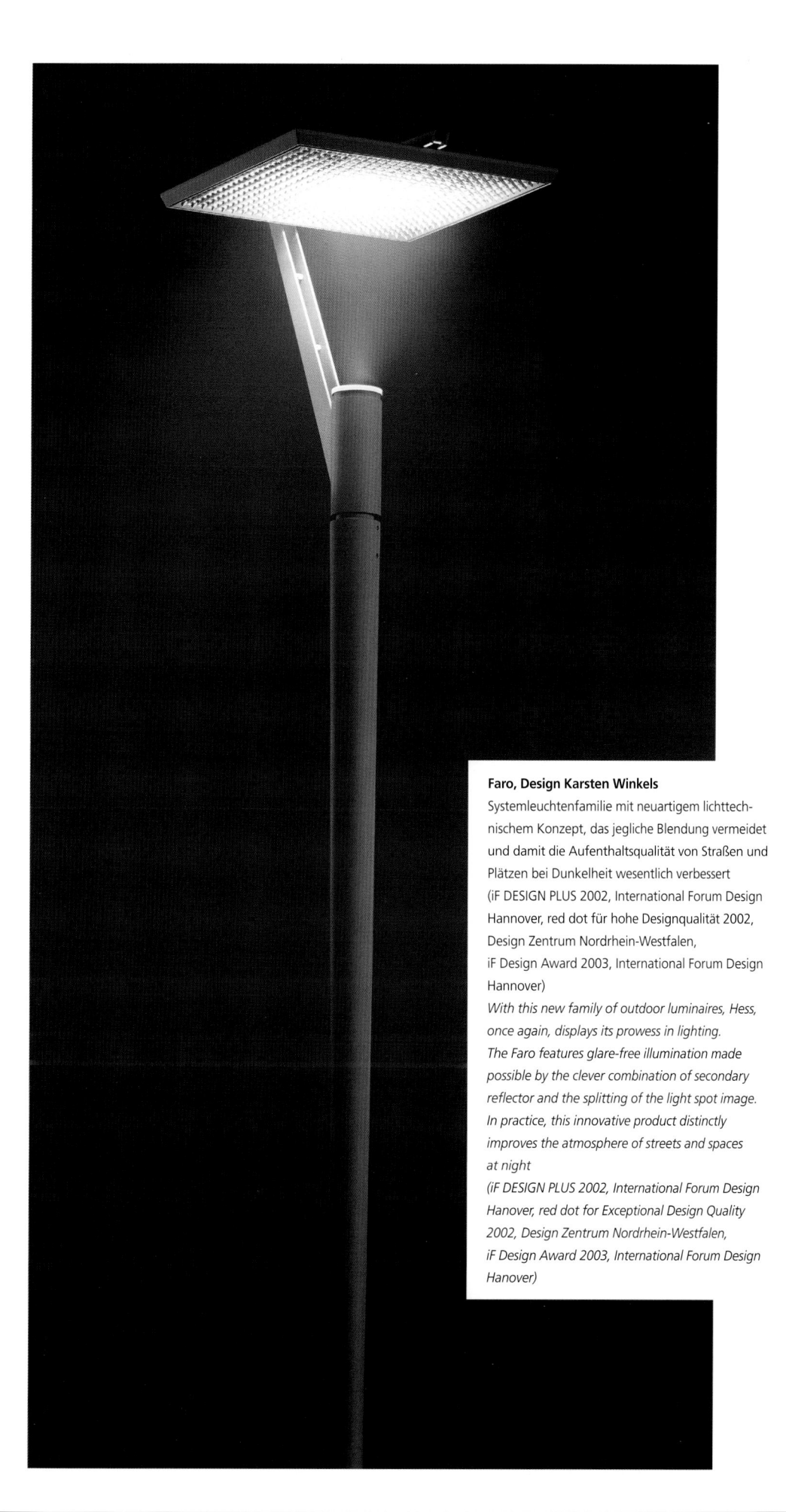

Hess Form + Licht is a leading manufacturer of decorative outdoor lighting for the international market. A widely diversified range of luminaires enables Hess Form + Licht to fulfil the specific requirements posed by demanding lighting design plans for public spaces, including object illumination. Architects, planners and real estate developers associate the Hess name with innovative lighting and high quality design. In addition, they value the functionality, practicality and durability of the products as well as the individualized project support. Besides its persistent further development of conventional illumination for streets, sidewalks and public spaces, Hess is very concerned with the potential offered by light as design element. Hess's ultra-modern LED and floodlighting technologies make extremely demanding lighting schemes possible in which architecture plays a central role. As a result, new dimensions of experience are created, which transform public spaces into living, unmistakable settings at night. Hess adds yet another significant contribution to the atmosphere and identity of spaces, pedestrian zones and parks with its outdoor furnishings, thereby providing greenery systems and street furniture that match its luminaires in form and design. Thus, Hess is one of the few manufacturers able to fulfil the requirements of truly comprehensive concepts for the design of urban and public areas.

Hawle Armaturen GmbH

Anschrift/*Address*
Liegnitzer Straße 6
D-83395 Freilassing

Ansprechpartner/*Contact*
Uwe Pickhardt

Telefon/*Phone*
+49 (0)8654/63 03-120

Telefax/*Fax*
+49 (0)8654/63 03-222

E-mail/*E-mail*
Uwe.Pickhardt@hawle.de

Internet/*Website*
www.hawle.de

Tätigkeitsfelder/*Fields of Activity*
Herstellung von Armaturen für Rohrnetze im Wasser-, Abwasser- und Gasbereich
Manufacturing instrument valves and manifolds for water lines, wastewater disposal systems and gas pipeline networks.

Funktionalität und Langlebigkeit – das sind die beiden Hauptkriterien, auf die bei Hawle Armaturen die gesamte Entwicklung und Produktion ausgerichtet ist. Nur damit kann den Armaturenanwendern eine langfristige Funktionssicherheit gewährleistet werden.

Aber nicht nur Qualität und Nachhaltigkeit zeichnet dieses Unternehmen aus, sondern auch Innovation. Hawle nahm sich als erster Hersteller der Entwicklung von Hydranten aus nichtrostenden Materialien an und setzt mit den gewindelosen Systemen BAIO und ZAK Maßstäbe in der Schwerarmaturentechnik.
Komplettiert wird das Armaturenangebot durch Hydranten, Regelventile, Klappen, Hausanschlüsse und Fittings.

Verarbeitungspräzision, moderne Oberflächenbeschichtung in Kombination mit funktionalen Verbindungssystemen für jede Rohrart sichern den Wasserarmaturen eine hohe Lebensdauer und lange Funktionsfähigkeit.
Precise workmanship, modern surface coating in combination with functional pipe connecting systems ensure a long life of the armature.

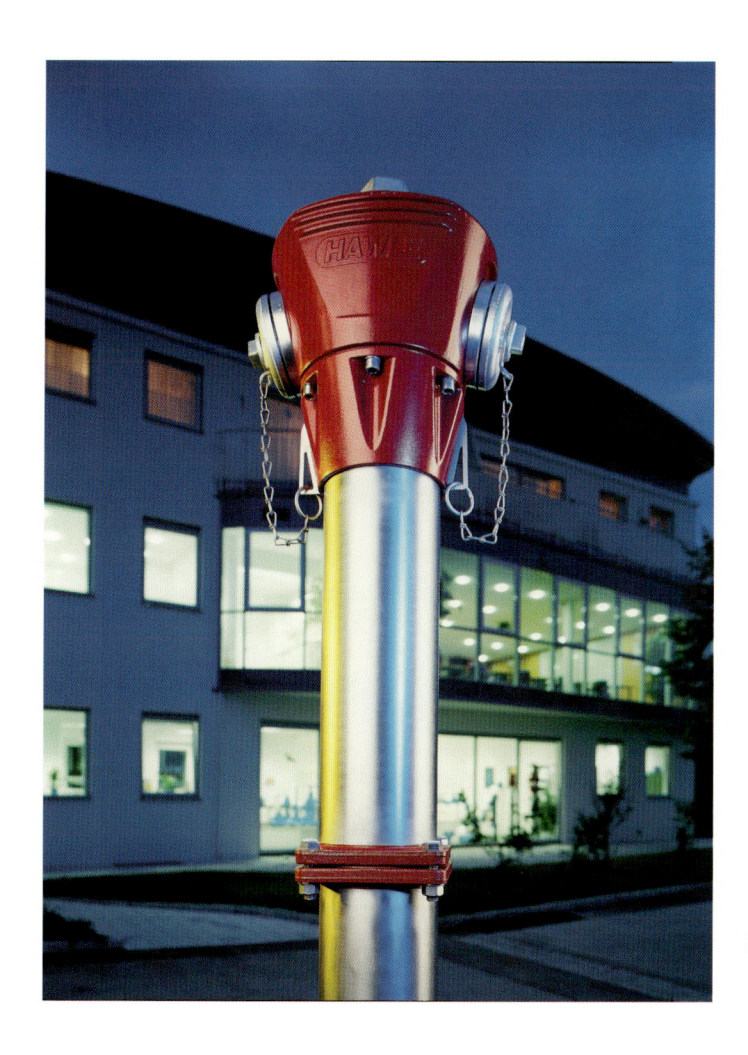

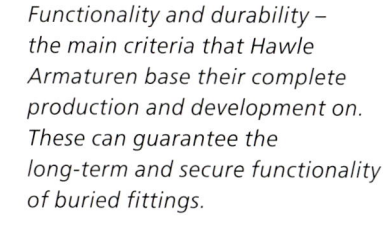

Functionality and durability – the main criteria that Hawle Armaturen base their complete production and development on. These can guarantee the long-term and secure functionality of buried fittings.

But the company not only stands for quality and sustainability, it also signifies innovation. Hawle was the first manufacturer that took the initiative for the development of the corrosion free hydrants and has set standards in the threadless pipe connecting technology with the BAIO and ZAK systems. The Hawle product range also includes flow control valves, butterfly valves, service connections and air release valves.

hawle

Design Award
iF
Winner 2001

Von einer Notwendigkeit zum optischen Anziehungspunkt des öffentlichen Lebens: Hydranten in ihrer schönsten Form.
From a basic necessity to an eye-catcher in public life: hydrants in its most superb shape.

Freizeit, Sport und Spiel
Leisure, Sport and Play

	Rang/*Rank*
BMW / D-München / 286 Punkte/*Points*	1
Minox / D-Wetzlar / 256 Punkte/*Points*	2
WOLF-Garten / D-Betzdorf / 228 Punkte/*Points*	3
Robert Bosch / D-München / 192 Punkte/*Points*	4
SRAM / D-Schweinfurt / 148 Punkte/*Points*	5
Fiskars Consumer / FIN-Billnäs / 144 Punkte/*Points*	6
SNIKE Sport / D-Stuttgart / 140 Punkte/*Points*	7
Pelikan / D-Hannover / 128 Punkte/*Points*	8
Elettromontaggi / I-Massa Martana / 72 Punkte/*Points*	9
AL-KO Geräte / D-Kötz / 64 Punkte/*Points*	10
ATIKA Maschinenfabrik / D-Ahlen / 64 Punkte/*Points*	10
Black Diamond / CH-Reinach / 64 Punkte/*Points*	10
Eschenbach Optik / D-Nürnberg / 64 Punkte/*Points*	10
Falke / D-Schmallenberg / 64 Punkte/*Points*	10
Hammarplast / S-Tingsryd / 64 Punkte/*Points*	10
Jørn Iversen Rødekro / DK-Rødekro / 64 Punkte/*Points*	10
Kaden & Kaden / D-Neuhausen / 64 Punkte/*Points*	10
Keppler & Fremer / D-Krefeld / 64 Punkte/*Points*	10
Kippy's Company / D-Sulz-Holzhausen / 64 Punkte/*Points*	10
Kleinebenne / D-Leopoldshöhe / 64 Punkte/*Points*	10
LINDBERG / DK-Abyhoj / 64 Punkte/*Points*	10
Manufactum / D-Waltrop / 64 Punkte/*Points*	10
Masterlock / USA-Milwaukee / 64 Punkte/*Points*	10
Möve / D-Berlin / 64 Punkte/*Points*	10
Puky / D-Wülfrath / 64 Punkte/*Points*	10
Stiga / D-Straelen / 64 Punkte/*Points*	10
Swarovski Optik / A-Absam / 64 Punkte/*Points*	10
TECTORY / D-Penzberg / 64 Punkte/*Points*	10
Treibholz / D-Düsseldorf / 64 Punkte/*Points*	10
Trico Sports / USA-Pacoima / 64 Punkte/*Points*	10
Tyrolia / A-Schwechat / 64 Punkte/*Points*	10
Urban Solutions / NL-Amsterdam / 64 Punkte/*Points*	10
Yamaha / J-Hamamatsu Shizuoka pref. / 64 Punkte/*Points*	10
Zwilling J.A. Henckels / D-Solingen / 64 Punkte/*Points*	10

BMW AG

Anschrift/*Address*
D-80788 München
Ansprechpartner/*Contact*
Abteilung Öffentlichkeitsarbeit
Public Relation Department
Telefon/*Phone*
+49 (0)89/38 20
Internet/*Website*
www.BMWgroup.de

Das Design der BMW Group ist für Menschen geschaffen, die auf der Suche nach einem präzisen Ausdruck ihrer mehrdimensionalen Identität sind. Individualisten, die niemals aufhören, die Bedeutung und das Sinnstiftende in dem, was sie tun und in dem, womit sie sich umgeben, zu erforschen. Dies gilt für die Designer und Ingenieure im Schaffensprozess ebenso wie für die Menschen, die diese Produkte besitzen.

The design of the BMW Group is created for people who are in search of a precise expression of their multidimensional identity. Individualists who never stop investigating the meaning of what they do and of the things they choose. This is valid for the designers and engineers in the creative process as well as for the people who use these products.

Weltweit verbinden die Menschen mit Automobilen, Motorrädern und Accessoires der BMW Group Qualität, Exklusivität und Innovation. Spitzenleistungen in Technik und Design verkörpert die BMW Group aus der Tradition heraus, denn gutes Design ist wegweisend und traditionsbewusst zugleich.
Es orientiert sich am Charakter der jeweiligen Marke und entwickelt sich beständig weiter, gutes Design bedeutet immer auch Fortschritt.

Worldwide people associate quality, exclusivity and innovation with automobiles, motorcycles and accessories of the BMW Group. Outstanding performance in technology and design is essential for BMW by its tradition, as good design is pioneering and tradition-minded at the same time. Good design always means progress and evolves around the character of the respective brand.

MINOX Fernoptik

Präzision auf kleinstem Raum

Die Ferne zum Greifen nah: auf Reisen, auf der Jagd oder bei anderen Freizeitvergnügen – mit den MINOX Ferngläsern behält man das Motiv immer im Auge. Aufgrund der jahrzehntelangen Erfahrung und dem Einsatz von modernsten Fertigungstechnologien setzt MINOX einen unvergleichlichen Standard in Zuverlässigkeit und Langlebigkeit. Mit seiner neuen Fernglas-Range stellt MINOX erneut alle Kompetenzen in feinmechanischer Präzision kombiniert mit einem erstklassigen Design unter Beweis.

So verbinden auch die vier neuen Ferngläser MINOX BD 8 x 32 BR asph., BD 8,5 x 42 BR asph., BD 10 x 42 BR asph. und BD 10 x 52 BR asph. eindrucksvoll die klassischen MINOX Werte: optische Höchstleistung und feinmechanische Präzision in kompakter Form. Zahlreiche funktionelle Innovationen machen sie zu Allroundern in der Anwendung – von der Bestimmung von Vögeln über die Wildbeobachtung bis zur Verfolgung von sportlichen Aktivitäten. Die verwendeten asphärischen Linsen bieten dem Benutzer eine kaum für möglich gehaltene Kontraststärke und Detailschärfe bis in den Randbereich. Eine nachprüfbare Spitzenleistung im Fernglasbau!

MINOX GmbH

Anschrift/*Address*
Walter-Zapp-Straße 4
D-35578 Wetzlar
Telefon/*Phone*
+49 (0)6441/917-0
Telefax/*Fax*
+49 (0)6441/917-612
E-mail/*E-mail*
info@minox.com
Internet/*Website*
www.minox.com
Mitarbeiter/*Employees*
30

BD 10 x 52 BR asph.

BD 8,5 x 42 BR asph.

BD 10 x 42 BR asph.

BD 8 x 32 BR asph.

MINOX sport optics

Legendary precision in the smallest format

Distant objects almost close enough to touch: whether travelling, hunting or practicing other leisure activities – with MINOX binoculars you can always keep objects in sight. Each MINOX product is the result of decades of experience with high performance optics and thanks to the modern product technologies, MINOX shares an incomparable standard of reliability and longevity. With its new binocular range, MINOX proves again the advantages of optical and mechanical precision combined with a first-class design.

The four new binoculars MINOX BD 8 x 32 BR asph., BD 8,5 x 42 BR asph., BD 10 x 42 BR asph. and BD 10 x 52 BR asph. combine the classic MINOX values: outstanding optical performance and precision engineering in a compact format. Their many innovative features and conveniences make them ideal for everything from bird watching and wildlife viewing to sporting events. The aspherical lenses of these binoculars enable high contrast intensity as well as an enormous sharpness of details right up to the edges. These are truly outstanding and versatile top-performance binoculars!

Freizeit, Sport und Spiel/ *Leisure, Sports and Play*

Fiskars

Fiskars Consumer Oy Ab

Anschrift/*Address*
FIN-10330 Billnäs
Telefon/*Phone*
+358 19/27 77 21
Telefax/*Fax*
+358 19/23 09 86
Gründungsdatum/*Foundation*
1649
Mitarbeiterzahl/*Employees*
600
Design-Team/*Design team*
7

Fiskars Consumer bietet Produkte für den Haus- und Gartenbereich an.

Als die älteste Industriefirma in Finnland (im Jahr 1649 gegründet) kombinieren unsere Produkte Tradition und Innovation mit einem reinen Design.

Ein gut funktionierendes Produkt spricht für sich selbst, ist offensichtlich und einfach. Aber idealerweise enthält es auch ein Rätsel, ein Geheimnis, das der Benutzer lösen muss, um in der Anwendung des Produkts eine positive Erfahrung zu machen.

Power Gear Heckenschere
Eine leichte Heckenschere mit patentierter, progressiver Doppelgetriebetechnik. Durch diesen Mechanismus verstärkt sich die Schneidkraft zum Ende der Schneidbewegung, wenn sie am meisten gebraucht wird. Dadurch wird eine Kraftersparnis von bis zu 35 % erreicht und die Belastung des Handgelenks, der Arme und Schultern wird wesentlich vermindert.

Power Gear Hedge Shear
Lightweight hedge shear based on a progressive, patented double gear mechanism. The cutting power increases towards the end of a cutting stroke where it is mainly needed. Compared to traditional designs, the required cutting force is less than 1/3. The stress on wrists, arms and shoulders is greatly reduced.

Fiskars Consumer offers products for both house and garden.

As the oldest industrial company in Finland (established in 1649) we combine long tradition with innovation and simplicity in design.

A well functioning product is self explanatory, obvious and simple. Ideally it also contains an enigma, a mystery for the user to solve, thus adding a positive experience to the use of the product.

Universalaxt
Der Axtkopf ist vom Stiel umschlossen, wodurch die Verbindung nicht gelockert, sondern Schlag für Schlag verstärkt wird. Breiteres Axtblatt zum Spalten und Trennen. Stiel in zwei verschiedenen Längen.

Universal Axe
Safe special fastening between head and handle ensures that the axe head will not come off. Wider blade design for splitting and cutting work. Available in two lengths.

Yamaha Corporation
Yamaha Product Design Laboratory

Anschrift/*Address*
10-1 Nakazawa-cho
Hamamatsu, Shizuoka
pref. 4308650 Japan
Ansprechpartner/*Contact*
Mr. Yasuhiro Kira
General Manager
of Product Design Laboratory
Telefon/*Phone*
+81 53-460-2883
Telefax/*Fax*
+81 53-463-4922
E-mail/*E-mail*
kira@pdl.yamaha.co.jp
Internet/*Website*
http://www.global.yamaha.com/
Gründungsdatum/*Foundation*
1887 Yamaha Corporation
1963 Product Design Laboratory
Mitarbeiter/*Employees*
6.239 Yamaha Corporation
24 Product Design Laboratory
Filiale/*Branch Office*
Yamahas globales Netzwerk umfasst Tochtergesellschaften und Joint Ventures in 20 Ländern in Nord- und Südamerika, Europa, Asien und Australien und betreibt Produktionsstätten an 15 Standorten in sieben Ländern.
Yamaha's global network spans subsidiaries and joint ventures in 20 countries in the Americas, Europe, Asia, and Australia, of which it has manufacturing facilities in 15 locations in seven countries.
Umsatz/*Turnover*
346.175 Millionen (Musikinstrumente: 48,5 %, andere: 51,5 %)
346,175 million (musical instruments: 48.5 %, others: 51.5 %)
Kunden/*Clients*
Unternehmensbereiche für Musikinstrumente, Audio-/Telekommunikationsgeräte, elektronische Geräte und andere
Divisions for musical instruments, audio and telecommunications equipment, electronic devices and others
Ausstattung/*Equipment*
Herstellung und Verkauf von Musikinstrumenten, Audio-/Telekommunikationsgeräten, elektronischen Geräten und anderen
Manufacture and sale of musical instruments, audio and telecommunications equipment, electronic devices and others
Tätigkeitsfelder/*Fields of Activity*
Musikinstrumente, Audio-/Telekommunikationsgeräte, Schallschutz, elektronische Geräte, Sportausstattung, Industrieausstattung, Musikerziehung usw.
Musical instruments, audio and telecommunications equipment, soundproofing work, electronic devices, sports equipment, industrial equipment, music education activities etc.

Unternehmensziel
Yamaha Corporation hat den Bereich „Sound/Musik und Multimedia" zum Kernpunkt ihrer Existenz gemacht, und wir betreiben unsere Aktivitäten mit dem Auftrag, „einen Beitrag dazu zu leisten, die Lebensqualität auf der ganzen Welt zu verbessern".

Corporate Objective
Yamaha Corporation places „sound/ music and multimedia" at the very core of its existence, and we pursue our corporate activities with a mission to „contribute to the enhancement of the quality of life around the world."

Yamaha Design-Philosophie
Wir haben 5 Schlüsselbegriffe.
- Integrität
- Innovativ
- Ästhetisch
- Unaufdringlich
- Soziale Verantwortung

Yamaha Design Philosophy
We have 5 Key words.
- *Integrity*
- *Innovative*
- *Aesthetic*
- *Unobtrusive*
- *Social Responsibility*

Yamaha
Music Production Synthesizer
(MOTIF7)
Dieses Spitzenmodell kombiniert High Quality Sound mit dem Gefühl auf der Bühne zu stehen.
This flagship model combines high quality sound production with on-stage appeal.
DESIGN INNOVATION `02 / Reddot Award - High Design Quality Germany

Die "EZ-EG"
Mittels eines einmaligen Lichtsystems macht diese Gitarre das Spielen einfach, mit oder ohne Begleitung.
Using a unique guide light system, this guitar makes playing easy, with or without accompaniment.
MONO MAGAZINE SUPER GOODS OF THE YEAR '02 / SILVER & Special prize Japan
SHIZUOKA GOOD DESIGN AWARDS '02 / Selection Japan

Yamaha
Silent Guitar SLG-100N
Der Aufbau des Rahmens, ohne
Resonanzkörper, ermöglicht das
Spielen - überall - zu jeder Zeit.
*The frame structure with
non-resonating body enables
performance anywhere and in
any environment.*
MONO MAGAZINE SUPER
GOODS OF THE YEAR '02 /
GOLD & Special prize
Japan

MAJOR AWARDS 1997-2001

SB7 Silent Brass
DESIGN INNOVATION '97 / Reddot
Award - Highest Design Quality,
Germany

DTX Silent Session Drum
DESIGN INNOVATION '97 / Reddot
Award - High Design Quality, Germany
THE CHICAGO ATHENAEUM '97 /
Permanent Collection, USA

SV-100 Silent Violin
THE CHICAGO ATHENAEUM '97 /
Permanent Collection, USA
DESIGN INNOVATION '98 / Reddot
Award - High Design Quality Germany
THE INTERNATIONAL DESIGN MAGA-
ZINE '98 / 44th Annual Design Review
- Design Distinction - Consumer Pro-
ducts, USA
iF Design Awards '99 / Most sought
after Design Award, Germany
Ranking:Design in Germany: Elected
on rank 9 from 100 ranks, Germany

WX5 Wind MIDI Controller
THE CHICAGO ATHENAEUM '98 /
Permanent Collection, USA
DESIGN INNOVATION '99 / Reddot
Award - High Design Quality, Germany
THE INTERNATIONAL DESIGN MAGA-
ZINE '99 / 45th Annual Design Review
- Design Distinction - Consumer
Products, USA
iF Design Awards '00 / Excellent
Design Award, Germany

SVC-200 Silent Cello / *compact type*
DESIGN INNOVATION '00 / Reddot
Award - Highest Design Quality,
Germany
THE INTERNATIONAL DESIGN MAGA-
ZINE '00 / 46th Annual Design Review
- Best of Category - Consumer
Products, USA
INDUSTRIAL DESIGN EXCELLENCE
AWARDS '00 / Bronze prize -
Consumer Products, USA
DIE NEUE SAMMLUNG '01 /
Permanent Collection, Germany

SLB-100 Silent Upright Bass
DESIGN INNOVATION '01 / Reddot
Award - High Design Quality, Germany

**MOTIF 7
(Music Production Synthesizer)**
DESIGN INNOVATION '02 / Reddot
Award - High Design Quality, Germany

Freizeit, Sport und Spiel/ *Leisure, Sports and Play*

Yamaha

10

Accessoires
Accessories

	Rang/*Rank*
Samsonite / B-Oudenaarde / 288 Punkte/*Points*	1
TROIKA Böll / D-Müschenbach / 212 Punkte/*Points*	2
Huser Feinmechanik / CH-Wettingen / 208 Punkte/*Points*	3
Ferdinand Menrad / D-Krailing / 208 Punkte/*Points*	3
Silhouette International Schmied / A-Linz / 208 Punkte/*Points*	3
Wilkinson Sword / D-Solingen / 192 Punkte/*Points*	6
BREE Collection / D-Isernhagen / 170 Punkte/*Points*	7
Rodenstock / D-München / 164 Punkte/*Points*	8
Gebr. Niessing / D-Vreden / 129 Punkte/*Points*	9
Bodensee Organisation Products / D-Meckenbeuren / 128 Punkte/*Points*	10

Accessoires/*Accessoires*

Rodenstock

Anschrift/*Address*
Isartalstraße 43
D-80469 München

Ansprechpartner/*Contact*
Jürgen Hopf
Presse- und Öffentlichkeitsarbeit
Press and Public Relation

Telefon/*Phone*
+49 (0)89/72 02-514

Telefax/*Fax*
+49 (0)89/72 02-226

E-mail/*E-mail*
presse@rodenstock.de

Internet/*Website*
www.rodenstock.de

Gründungsdatum/*Foundation*
1877

Mitarbeiter/*Employees*
rund 5.800 Mitarbeiter
(2001, weltweit)
*approx. 5,800 employees
(2001, worldwide)*

Tochtergesellschaften/
Subsidiaries
Australien, Chile, Deutschland, Frankreich, Großbritannien, Italien, Japan, Kanada, Malta, Niederlande, Norwegen, Österreich, Polen, Schweden, Schweiz, Thailand, Tschechische Republik, Uruguay, USA

Umsatz/*Turnover*
422 Mio. € (2001, weltweit)
422 million € (2001, worldwide)

Kunden/*Clients*
ca. 9.000 Augenoptikbetriebe allein in Deutschland; weltweit ein Vielfaches davon
approx. 9,000 optician companies in Germany, worldwide multiple

Tätigkeitsfelder/*Fields of Activity*
Entwicklung, Herstellung und Vertrieb von Brillen, Brillengläsern und Brillenfassungen
Development, production and distribution of spectacles, spectacle glasses and frames

„Sehen" und „Gesicht" – zwei Begriffe, die unmittelbar miteinander verknüpft sind. Ganz egal, ob wir unser „Gesicht wahren", jemandem „wie aus dem Gesicht geschnitten" sind, unser „wahres Gesicht zeigen" oder unser „Gesicht verlieren" - immer dann, wenn es um die Einschätzung der Persönlichkeit durch andere geht, spielen das Sehen und das Gesicht eine Schlüsselrolle.

Gutes Brillendesign bedeutet für Rodenstock daher vor allem, nicht unser Produkt, sondern das Gesicht seines Trägers in den Mittelpunkt zu stellen. Mit Brillen, die sich weder als extravagante Modeartikel noch als bloße Sehhilfen verstehen, sondern als Ausdrucksmittel individuellen Stils. Ästhetische Accessoires, die – weil uns die Augen wichtiger sind als die Brille – die Physiognomie unterstreichen und nicht dominieren. Kurz: Brillen für Leute, denen ihr gutes Sehen und Aussehen genau so wichtig ist wie uns.

Ultraflache Brillenfassung R 4382 mit schraubenlosem Scharnier
Ultra-slim frame R 4382 with no-screw hinge

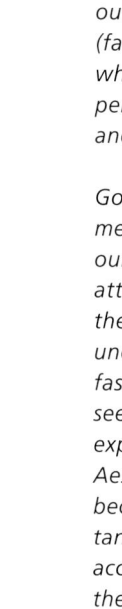

"Seeing" and "face" – two concepts that are bound together. Regardless of whether we "save our face", "is a spitting image (face)" of someone or "lose face", whether the assessment of a personality by another, the seeing and the face play a key role.

Good spectacles design therefore means for Rodenstock not placing our product in the center of attention but rather the face of the wearer. Spectacles are to be understood neither as extravagant fashion article nor as a simple seeing aid, but rather means of expression of individual style. Aesthetic accessoires, which – because the eyes are more important to us than the spectacles – accentuate and do not dominate the physiognomy.
In short: these are spectacles for people for whom looking good and seeing properly are just as important as for us.

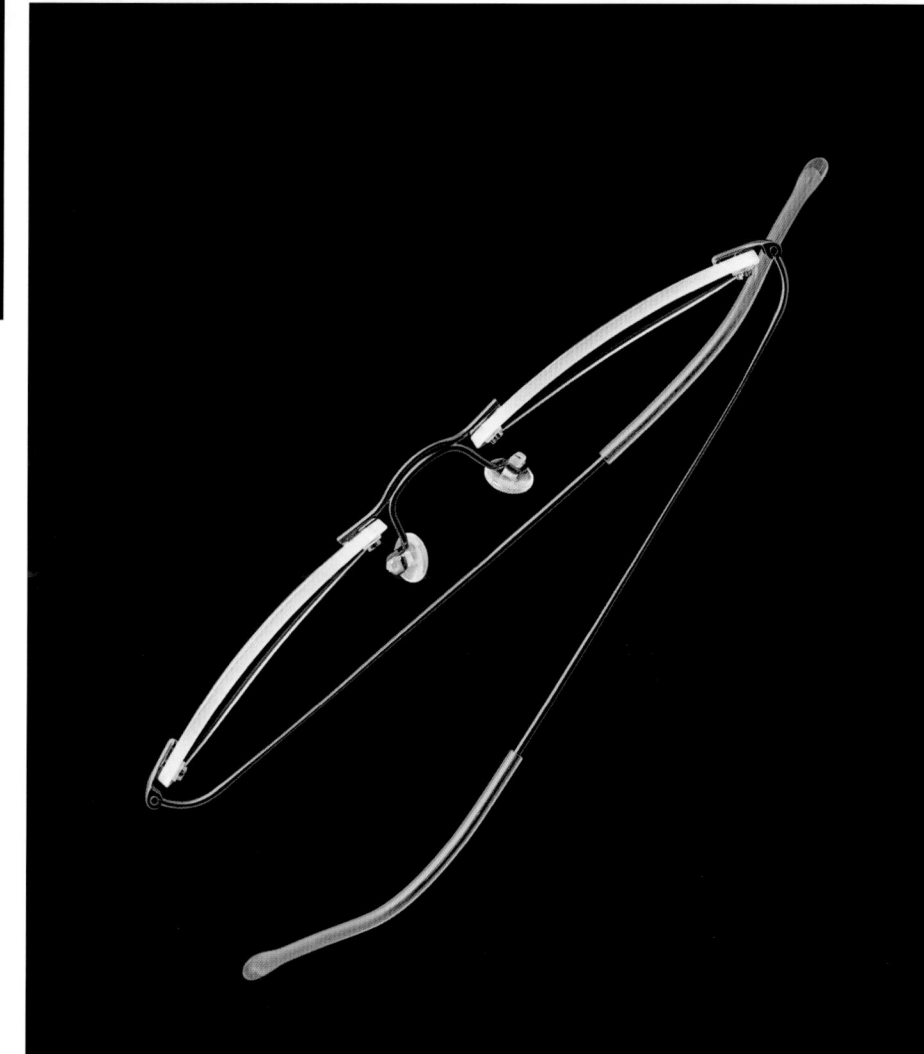

Gesamt-Ranking: Top 20
Overall Ranking: Top 20

Rang/*Rank*

IBM / D-Herrenberg / 1424 Punkte/*Points*	1
Sony Europe / D-Berlin / 1376 Punkte/*Points*	2
Festo / D-Denkendorf / 1259 Punkte/*Points*	3
Siemens-Electrogeräte / D-München / 938 Punkte/*Points*	4
BMW / D-München / 898 Punkte/*Points*	5
Samsung Electronics / D-Schwalbach / 712 Punkte/*Points*	6
Heidelberger Druckmaschinen / D-Heidelberg / 562 Punkte/*Points*	7
Viessmann Werke / D-Allendorf / 554 Punkte/*Points*	8
SPECTRAL GESELLSCHAFT FÜR LICHTTECHNIK / D-Freiburg / 528 Punkte/*Points*	9
Loewe Opta / D-Kronach / 526 Punkte/*Points*	10
Sharp Electronic / D-Hamburg / 520 Punkte/*Points*	11
Canon / D-Krefeld / 512 Punkte/*Points*	12
Gira Giersiepen / D-Radevormwald / 493 Punkte/*Points*	13
Artemide / D-Fröndenberg / 485 Punkte/*Points*	14
imperial-Werke / D-Bünde / 464 Punkte/*Points*	15
Siemens / D-München / 456 Punkte/*Points*	16
MABEG Kreuschner / D-Soest / 452 Punkte/*Points*	17
Robert Bosch / D-München / 448 Punkte/*Points*	18
Philips / NL-Eindhoven / 448 Punkte/*Points*	18
Sedus Stoll / D-Waldshut / 448 Punkte/*Points*	18

Festo AG & Co. KG
Corporate Design

Anschrift/*Address*
Rechbergstraße 3
D-73770 Denkendorf
Ansprechpartner/*Contact*
Prof. Dipl.-Ing. Axel Thallemer
Head of Corporate Design
Telefon/*Phone*
+49(0)711/3 47 38 80
Telefax/*Fax*
+49(0)711/3 47 38 99
E-mail/*E-mail*
tem@festo.com

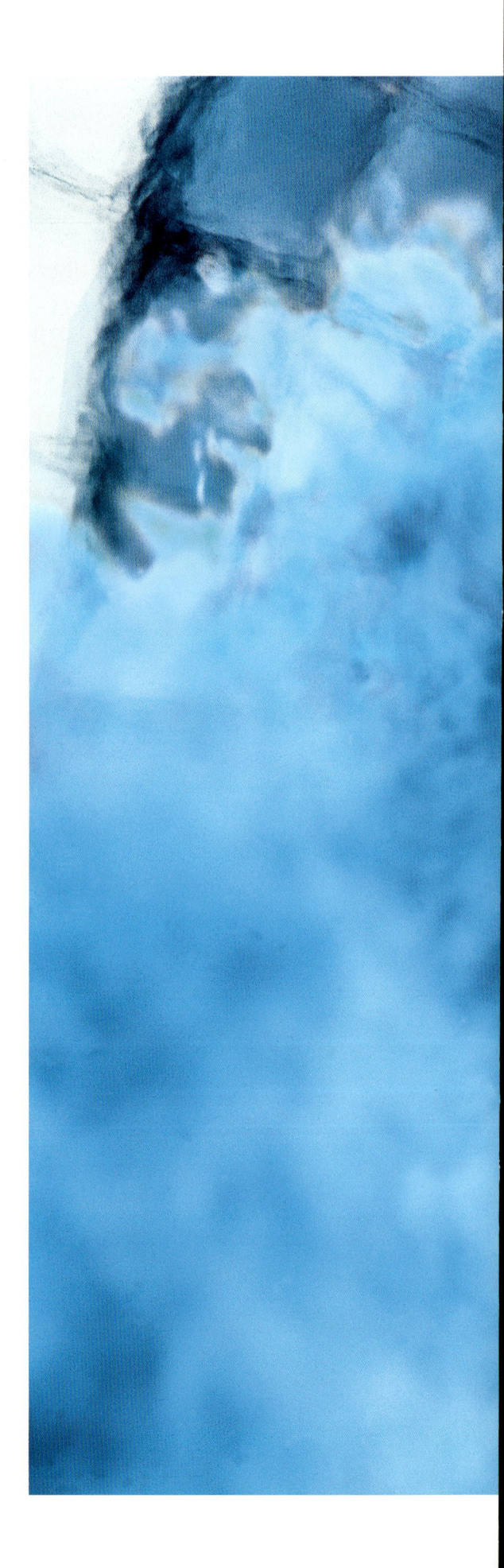

Gesamt-Ranking: Top 20 / Overall Ranking: Top 20

Festo 3

Siemens-Electrogeräte GmbH
Designabteilung (MDS)

Anschrift/*Address*
Postfach 10 02 50
D-80076 München
Ansprechpartner/*Contact*
Gerd E. Wilsdorf
Telefon/*Phone*
+49 (0)89/45 90-32 35
Telefax/*Fax*
+49 (0)89/45 90-298
Mitarbeiter/*Employees*
12

„Unsere Geräte können es sich nicht leisten, nur kurz an der Oberfläche des Zeitgeistes zu schwimmen. Sie müssen ihre inneren Werte formal ehrlich und optisch langlebig dokumentieren. Ein Herd ist kein kurzlebiger Konsumartikel, er ist ein langfristiges Investitionsgut für die Küche. Dementsprechend sind ehrliche Materialien sowie Disziplin und Eindeutigkeit in der Gestaltung die erklärten Ziele des Siemens Designs."

Gerd E. Wilsdorf,
Chefdesigner
der Siemens-Electrogeräte GmbH

Premium Kleingeräte-Serie
Premium small appliance series
TT 91100, TC 91100, TW 91199
Design: F.A. Porsche für Siemens

"Our appliances cannot afford to float briefly in the surface of fashion. They have to document their inner values formerly, honestly and optically over a long service life. A cooker is not a short-term consumer article, it is a long-term investment for the kitchen. Accordingly, honest materials as well as discipline and unambiguous styling are the declared goals of Siemens design."

Gerd E. Wilsdorf,
Chief Designer
of Siemens-Electrogeräte GmbH

Funktionseinheit Kochen mit
Einbauherd der **s-line**®
*Functional unit with **s-line**®*
built-in cooker
HE 68 E 57, EK 74754, LC 66671
Design: Gerd E. Wilsdorf

Hall of Fame
Hersteller/*Manufacturer*

					Platzierungen/*Placements* 1997–2003	Gesamt-punkte/*Total points*	Rang/*Rank*
1997/98 🔵	1998/99 🟡	1999/00 🟣	2001/02 🟤	2002/03 🔴			

Handwerk und Industrie/
Trade and Industry

Manufacturer	1997/98	1998/99	1999/00	2001/02	2002/03	Total points	Rank
Festo / D-Denkendorf	🔵	🟡	🟣	🟤	🔴	4779	1
Viessmann Werke / D-Allendorf			🟣	🟤		1474	2
Robert Bosch / D-Stuttgart	🔵	🟡	🟣			1152	3
Hilti / FL-Schaan	🔵	🟡	🟣		🔴	958	4
Heidelberger Druckmaschinen / D-Heidelberg	🔵				🔴	648	5
wolfcraft / D-Kempenich			🟣	🟤		520	6
Siemens / D-München		🟡	🟣			426	7
Fluke Industrial / NL-Almelo	🔵					392	8
WOLF-Garten / D-Betzdorf		🟡				368	9
C. & E. Fein / D-Stuttgart				🟤	🔴	320	10

Medizin und Rehabilitation/
Medicine and Rehabilitation

Manufacturer	1997/98	1998/99	1999/00	2001/02	2002/03	Total points	Rank
Olympus Winter & Ibe / D-Hamburg	🔵			🟤	🔴	760	1
Siemens / D-München			🟣	🟤	🔴	512	2
designafairs / D-München	🔵					466	3
Philips / NL-Eindhoven	🔵			🟤		442	4
B. Braun Melsungen / D-Melsungen			🟣	🟤		368	5
Deutsches Rotes Kreuz / D-Nottuln			🟣	🟤		300	6
Medeqo-Thermamed / D-Bad Oeynhausen				🟤		288	7
Carl Zeiss / D-Oberkochen		🟡		🟤		284	8
IKA Analysentechnik / D-Heitersheim	🔵	🟡				222	9
Dräger Medizintechnik / D-Lübeck	🔵					200	10

Medien, Kommunikation und Unterhaltungselektronik/
Media, Communication and Entertainment Electronics

Firma	B	G	L	O	R	Wert	Rang
Sony Europe / D-Berlin	●	●	●	●	●	4448	1
IBM / D-Herrenberg	●	●		●	●	3640	2
Loewe / D-Kronach	●	●	●	●	●	2182	3
Philips / NL-Eindhoven	●	●	●	●	●	1728	4
Siemens / D-München		●	●	●	●	1554	5
Samsung Electronics / D-Schwalbach				●	●	1008	6
Sharp Electronic / D-Hamburg				●	●	976	7
Canon / D-Krefeld	●		●		●	960	8
Apple Computer / D-Feldkirchen		●	●		●	840	9
Grundig / D-Fürth	●			●		969	10

Verkehrsmittel und Sonderfahrzeuge/
Transportation and Special Use Vehicles

Firma	B	G	L	O	R	Wert	Rang
BMW / D-München	●	●	●	●	●	1606	1
DaimlerChrysler / D-Sindelfingen	●	●	●	●	●	1295	2
Audi / D-Ingolstadt	●	●	●	●	●	1090	3
Volkswagen / D-Wolfsburg	●	●	●	●		862	4
Dr. Ing. h.c. F. Porsche / D-Stuttgart	●		●	●	●	518	5
Recaro / D-Kirchheim-Tek	●	●	●			402	6
Bomag / D-Boppard am Rhein	●	●	●			300	7
Siemens DUEWAG / D-Krefeld					●	294	8
Crown Gabelstapler / D-München					●	256	9
Honda / D-Offenbach	●				●	224	10

Büro und Objekt/
Office and Public Space

Firma	B	G	L	O	R	Wert	Rang
SPECTRAL GES. FÜR LICHTTECHNIK / D-Freiburg		●	●	●	●	1532	1
Kusch + Co. Sitzmöbelwerke / D-Hallenberg	●	●	●			1372	2
Gebrüder Thonet / D-Frankenberg		●	●	●	●	1076	3
Wilkhahn Wilkening + Hahne / D-Bad Münder	●	●	●		●	898	4
Fritz Hansen / DK-Allerød	●	●			●	762	5
Sedus Stoll / D-Waldshut			●		●	712	6
Vorwerk / D-Wuppertal	●			●		576	7
iGuzzini / D-Planegg	●				●	544	8
Unifor / I-Turate	●				●	440	9
Tobias Grau / D-Hamburg	●	●				406	10

Hall of Fame
Hersteller/*Manufacturer*

1997/98 ● (teal) 1998/99 ● (yellow) 1999/00 ● (purple) 2001/02 ● (ochre) 2002/03 ● (red)

Platzierungen/*Placements* 1997–2003 | Gesamtpunkte/*Total points* | Rang/*Rank*

Wohnung/
Living

Manufacturer	1997/98	1998/99	1999/00	2001/02	2002/03	Total points	Rank
nya nordiska / D-Dannenberg	●	●	●	●	●	1360	1
Gira Giersiepen / D-Radevormwald			●		●	726	2
ClassiCon / D-München		●		●	●	576	3
Moormann Möbel / D-Aschau	●	●		●	●	566	4
Artemide / D-Fröndenberg				●	●	361	5
COR Sitzmöbel / D-Rheda-Wiedenbrück	●			●		312	6
Belux / CH-Wohlen	●			●		308	7
FSB Franz Schneider Brakel / D-Brakel			●	●		294	8
Roset / D-Gundelfingen			●		●	256	9
Lattoflex Karl Thomas Möbelwerkstätten / D-Bremervörde	●		●			242	10

Haushalt, Küche und Bad/
Household, Kitchen and Bathroom

Manufacturer	1997/98	1998/99	1999/00	2001/02	2002/03	Total points	Rank
Siemens Electrogeräte / D-München	●	●	●	●	●	3390	1
Robert Bosch Hausgeräte / D-München		●	●	●	●	1556	2
Authentics artipresent / D-Holzgerlingen	●	●	●			1526	3
imperial-Werke / D-Bünde			●	●	●	1418	4
Hansgrohe / D-Schiltach	●	●	●		●	1364	5
WMF / D-Geislingen	●	●		●	●	1158	6
Miele & Cie. / D-Gütersloh	●			●	●	984	7
Philips / NL-Eindhoven	●	●	●			920	8
Hoesch Metall + Kunststoffwerk / D-Düren			●	●	●	918	9
Leonardo-glaskoch / D-Bad Driburg			●	●	●	896	10

Public Design/
Public Design

Company	Blue	Yellow	Purple	Gold	Red	Score	Rank
MABEG Kreuschner / D-Soest		●	●	●	●	836	1
Hess Form + Licht / D-Villingen-Schwenningen			●	●	●	668	2
BEGA Gantenbrink-Leuchten / D-Menden	●		●	●		576	3
ERCO Leuchten / D-Lüdenscheid			●	●		424	4
Leitner / D-Waiblingen		●		●	●	400	5
Interflex Datensysteme / D-Stuttgart		●		●		362	6
DZ Licht / D-Fröndenberg	●	●				278	7
Burkhardt Leitner constructiv / D-Stuttgart		●				264	8
Stadler Projekt / D-Offenbach	●					192	9
Wall / D-Berlin					●	192	9
Willy Meyer + Sohn / D-Hemer					●	192	9

Freizeit, Sport und Spiel/
Leisure, Sports and Play

Company	Blue	Yellow	Purple	Gold	Red	Score	Rank
BMW / D-München		●		●	●	676	1
WOLF-Garten / D-Betzdorf			●	●	●	628	2
Yamaha / J-Hamamatsu Shizuoka pref.	●	●	●	●	●	544	3
Minox / D-Wetzlar	●	●			●	440	4
SRAM / D-Schweinfurt	●			●	●	396	5
Deutsche Angelgeräte Manufaktur / D-Gunzenhausen	●	●	●			320	6
Pelikan / D-Hannover		●			●	310	7
Fiskars Consumer / FIN-Billnäs	●			●	●	296	8
Naef / CH-Zeiningen		●	●			200	9
THM Faserverbundtechnologie / D-Alt Duvestedt		●	●			200	9

Accessoires/
Accessoires

Company	Blue	Yellow	Purple	Gold	Red	Score	Rank
BREE Collection / D-Isernhagen	●	●	●	●	●	1240	1
Gebr. Niessing / D-Vreden	●	●	●	●	●	801	2
Rodenstock / D-München	●		●	●	●	714	3
Samsonite / B-Oudenaarde	●	●	●		●	688	4
Meister + Co. / D-Radolfzell	●			●		456	5
Silhouette International Schmied / A-Linz			●	●	●	416	6
TROIKA Böll / D-Müschenbach		●	●		●	396	7
Ferdinand Menrad / D-Krailing		●	●		●	378	8
Watch People / D-Rheine			●	●		360	9
C. Josef Lamy / D-Heidelberg		●	●			320	10

Adressen Hersteller/
Addresses Manufacturers

AEG Hausgeräte GmbH
Muggenhofer Straße 135
90429 Nürnberg

Ulrich Alber GmbH + Co. KG
Sigmaringer Straße 100
72548 Albstadt

AL-KO Geräte GmbH
Ichenhauser Straße 14
89359 Kötz

Apple Computer GmbH
Dornacher Straße 3d
85622 Feldkirchen

Artemide
Hans-Böckler-Straße 2
58730 Fröndenberg
Seiten/*Pages* 108/109

**ATIKA Maschinenfabrik
Wilhelm Pollmeier GmbH & Co.**
Schinkelstraße 97
59227 Ahlen

Audi AG
Postfach
85045 Ingolstadt

BAHCO BELZER GmbH
Hastener Straße 4
42349 Wuppertal

Balzers Verschleißschutz GmbH
Am Ockenheimer Graben 41
55411 Bingen-Kempten

**Bauerfeind
Orthopädie GmbH & Co. KG**
Arnoldstraße 15
47906 Kempen

Black Diamond Europe
Christoph-Merian-Ring 7
CH-4153 Reinach

BMW AG
80788 München
Seiten/*Pages* 34/35, 62/63, 100/101, 140/141

**Bodensee Organisation Products
GmbH & Co. KG**
Am Degelbach 1
88071 Meckenbeuren

Bombardier Transportation
Saatwinkler Damm 43
13627 Berlin

Robert Bosch Hausgeräte GmbH
Hochstraße 17
81669 München
Seiten/*Pages* 52/53, 122/123

BREE Collection GmbH & Co. KG
Gerberstraße 3
30916 Isernhagen

British Airways PLC
Waterside PO Box 365
GB-UB7 0GB Harmondsworth

Canon Inc.
Europapark Fichtenhain A10
47807 Krefeld

**Carpet Concept
Objekt-Teppichboden GmbH**
Bunzlauer Straße 7
33719 Bielefeld

ClassiCon GmbH
Sigmund-Riefler-Bogen 3
81379 München

Crown Gabelstapler GmbH
Moosacher Straße 52
80809 München
Seiten/*Pages* 36/37

DaimlerChrysler AG
71059 Sindelfingen

Karl Dungs GmbH & Co.
Siemensstraße 6-10
73660 Urbach

Elettromontaggi S.R.L.
Loc Colle 91/a
I-06056 Massa Martana

**Eschenbach Optik
GmbH + Co.**
Schopenhauer Straße 10
90409 Nürnberg

EVA Deutschland
Pinneberger Chaussee 99
25436 Moorrege

Falke KG
Oststraße 5a
57392 Schmallenberg

**C. & E. Fein
GmbH & Co. KG**
Leuschnerstraße 41-47
70176 Stuttgart

Ferag AG
Zürichstraße 74
CH-8340 Hinwil

Festo AG & Co.
Rechbergstraße 3
73770 Denkendorf
Seiten/*Pages* 20/21, 74/75, 90/91, 154/155

Fiskars Consumer Oy AB
FIN-10330 Billnäs
Seiten/*Pages* 144/155

Ganymed GmbH
Breitenloh 7
82335 Berg/Starnberger See
Seiten/*Pages* 28/29

**Gira Giersiepen
GmbH & Co. KG**
Dahlienstraße
42477 Radevormwald
Seiten/*Pages* 106/107

Hammarplast AB
Box 6
S-36221 Tingsryd

**Hankook Reifen
Deutschland GmbH**
Hauptstraße 47
63303 Dreieich

Fritz Hansen A/S
Allerødvej 8
DK-3450 Allerød

Hansgrohe AG
Auestraße 5-9
77761 Schiltach

Paul Hartmann AG
Paul-Hartmann-Straße 12
89522 Heidenheim

Hawle Armaturen
Liegnitzer Straße 6
83395 Freilassing
Seiten/*Pages* 136/137

Heidelberger Druckmaschinen AG
Speyerer Straße 4
69115 Heidelberg

Hess Form + Licht GmbH
Schlachthausstraße 19
78050 Villingen-Schwenningen
Seiten/*Pages* 134/135

Hilti AG
Feldkircherstraße 100
FL-9494 Schaan

**Hoesch Metall + Kunststoffwerk
GmbH & Co.**
Postfach 10 04 24
52304 Düren
Seiten/*Pages* 128/129

**Honda Motor Europe
(North) GmbH**
Sprendlinger Landstraße 166
63069 Offenbach

Huser Feinmechanik AG
Kirchstraße 2
CH-5430 Wettingen

IBM Deutschland GmbH
Am Fichtenberg 1
71083 Herrenberg

iGuzzini Deutschland GmbH
Bunsenstraße 5
82152 Planegg

imperial-Werke oHG
Borries-/Installstraße 10-18
32257 Bünde
Seiten/*Pages* 120/121

**interlübke Gebr. Lübke
GmbH & Co. KG**
Ringstraße 145
33378 Rheda-Wiedenbrück

Iomega International S.A.
12, Avenue de Morgines
CH-1213 Petit-Laney 1

Jørn Iversen Rødekro aps.
Hydevadvej 48
DK-6230 Rødekro

Jaguar Deutschland GmbH
Frankfurter Straße
61476 Kronberg

Kaden & Kaden Holzgestaltung
Schützenhausweg 3
09544 Neuhausen

Alfred Kärcher GmbH & Co.
Alfred-Kärcher-Straße 28-40
71364 Winnenden

Keppler & Fremer GmbH
Weggenhofstraße 27
47798 Krefeld

**Kippy's Company
Golf- und Sportartikel**
Heubergstraße 2
72172 Sulz-Holzhausen

**Kleinebenne GmbH
Patria Markenfahrräder**
Hansastraße 20
33813 Leopoldshöhe

Leitner GmbH
Düsseldorfer Straße 14
71332 Waiblingen

Leonardo-glaskoch
Industriegebiet Herste
33014 Bad Driburg

LINDBERG A/S
Frichsparken 40c
DK-8230 Abyhoj

Loewe AG
Industriestraße 11
96317 Kronach

MABEG Kreuschner GmbH & Co. KG
Ferdinand-Gabriel-Weg 10
59494 Soest

Manufactum Produkt GmbH
Zeche Waltrop
45731 Waltrop

Masterlock
2600 North 32nd Street
USA-WI 53219 Milwaukee

**Matsushita Communication
Industrial UK Ltd.**
Daytona Drive Colthrop
GB-RG 19 ZD Thatchham, Berkshire

Ferdinand Menrad GmbH+Co.KG
Oderstraße 2
73522 Schwäbisch Gmünd

Merten GmbH & Co. KG
Fritz-Kotz-Straße 8
51674 Wiehl

Metabowerke GmbH & Co.
Postfach 1229
72602 Nürtingen

Willy Meyer + Sohn GmbH + Co. KG
Sternmessiepener Weg 5
58675 Hemer

Microsoft GmbH
Einsteinstraße 12
85716 Unterschleißheim

Miele & Cie. GmbH & Co.
Carl-Miele-Straße 29
33332 Gütersloh
Seiten/*Pages* 54/55, 130/131

Minox GmbH
Walter-Zapp-Straße 4
35578 Wetzlar
Seiten/*Pages* 142/143

**Möve Frottana
Textil GmbH & Co. KG**
Kaiser-Friedrich-Straße 90
10585 Berlin

Moormann Möbel GmbH
An der Festhalle 2
83229 Aschau

Multi-Contact Essen GmbH
Hövelstraße 214
45326 Essen

Gebr. Niessing GmbH & Co.
Butenwall 117
48691 Vreden

nya nordiska textiles gmbh
An den Ratswiesen
29451 Dannenberg
Seiten/*Pages* 42/43, 110/111

Olympus Winter & Ibe GmbH
Kuehnstraße 61
22045 Hamburg

**Pelikan Vertriebsgesellschaft
mbH & Co. KG**
Podbielskistraße 141
30177 Hannover

Pharmacia GmbH
Am Wolfsmantel 46
91058 Erlangen

Dr. Ing. h.c. F. Porsche AG
Porscheplatz 1
70435 Stuttgart

Puky GmbH & Co. KG
Fortunastraße 11
42489 Wülfrath

Renfert GmbH
Industriegebiet
78274 Hilzingen

Rodenstock GmbH
Isartalstraße 43
80469 München
Seiten/*Pages* 150/151

Roset Möbel GmbH
Industriestraße 51
79194 Gundelfingen/Freiburg

Georg Schlegel GmbH & Co.
Am Kapellenweg 3
88525 Dürmentingen
Seiten/*Pages* 92/93

Schmitz-Werke GmbH + Co
Hansestraße 87
48282 Emsdetten
Seiten/*Pages* 112/113

Sharp Electronic (Europe) GmbH
Sonninstraße 3
20097 Hamburg

Siemens AG
Wittelsbacher Platz 2
80333 München

Siemens DUEWAG
Duisburger Straße 145
47823 Krefeld

Siemens-Electrogeräte GmbH
Hochstraße 17
81669 München
Seiten/*Pages* 48/49, 50/51, 116/117, 156/157

Sirona Dental Systems GmbH
Fabrikstraße 31
64623 Bensheim

SMC Pneumatic GmbH
Boschring 13-15
63329 Egelsbach

Sony Europe GmbH
Kemperplatz 1
10785 Berlin

**SPECTRAL GESELLSCHAFT
FÜR LICHTTECHNIK mbH**
Bötzinger Straße 31
79111 Freiburg im Breisgau

Stiga GmbH
Albert-Steeger-Straße 28
47638 Straelen

Still GmbH
Berzeliusstraße 10
22113 Hamburg

Swarovski Optik KG
Swarovskistraße 70
A-6067 Absam

**TECTORY
Technik mit Design GmbH**
Sindelsdorfer Straße 66
82377 Penzberg

Thermamed GmbH
Kirchstraße 8
32547 Bad Oeynhausen

Gebrüder Thonet GmbH
Michael-Thonet-Straße 1
35066 Frankenberg

Treibholz GmbH
Planetenstraße 1
40223 Düsseldorf

Trico Sports Inc.
13541 Desmond Street
USA-91331-2316 Pacoima, California

TROIKA Böll GmbH & Co. KG
Nisterfeld 11
57629 Müschenbach

Tyrolia HTM Sport- und Freizeitgeräte
Tyroliaplatz 1
A-2320 Schwechat

ufo unbegrenzt flexible Objekte GmbH
Hans-Böckler-Straße 20
30851 Langenhagen

Unifor S.p.A.
Via Isonzo 1
I-22078 Turate (Como)

Urban Solutions BV
KNSM-Laan 117
NL-1919 LB Amsterdam

Viessmann Werke GmbH & Co.
Industriestraße 5
35108 Allendorf
Seiten/*Pages* 118/119

Vitra GmbH
Charles-Eames-Straße 2
79576 Weil am Rhein

Vollmer Werke Maschinenfabrik
Ehinger Straße 34
88400 Biberach / Riss

MIWE Michael Wenz GmbH
Michael-Wenz-Straße 2-10
97450 Arnstein

Wilkhahn
Wilkening + Hahne GmbH + Co.
Fritz-Hahne-Straße 8
31848 Bad Münder

WMF Württembergische Metallwarenfabrik AG
Eberhardstraße
73309 Geislingen/Steige
Seiten/*Pages* 124/125, 126/127

WOLF-Garten GmbH & Co KG
Industriestraße
57518 Betzdorf

Yamaha Corporation Japan
10-1 Nakazawa-cho
J-Hamamatsu Shizuoka
pref. 430-8650
Seiten/*Pages* 146/147

alfi Zitzmann GmbH
Ernst-Abbe-Straße 14
97877 Wertheim

Zwilling J.A. Henckels AG
Grünewalder Straße 14-22
42657 Solingen

Alle Abbildungen mit freundlicher Genehmigung der Designer und Hersteller.
All pictures with the kind permission of designers and manufacturers.